IMMERSION
Bible Studies

COLOSSIANS,
1 & 2 THESSALONIANS

D1157362

Praise for IMMERSION

"IMMERSION BIBLE STUDIES is a powerful tool in helping readers to hear God speak through Scripture and to experience a deeper faith as a result."
Adam Hamilton, author of *24 Hours That Changed the World*

"This unique Bible study makes Scripture come alive for students. Through the study, students are invited to move beyond the head into the heart of faith."
Bishop Joseph W. Walker, author of *Love and Intimacy*

"If you're looking for a deeper knowledge and understanding of God's Word, you must dive into IMMERSION BIBLE STUDIES! Whether in a group setting or as an individual, you will experience God and his unconditional love for each of us in a whole new way."
Pete Wilson, founding and senior pastor of Cross Point Church

"This beautiful series helps readers become fluent in the words and thoughts of God, for purposes of illumination, strength building, and developing a closer walk with the One who loves us so."
Laurie Beth Jones, author of *Jesus, CEO* and *The Path*

"I highly commend to you IMMERSION BIBLE STUDIES, which tells us what the Bible teaches and how to apply it personally."
John Ed Mathison, author of *Treasures of the Transformed Life*

"The IMMERSION BIBLE STUDIES series is no less than a game changer. It ignites the purpose and power of Scripture by showing us how to do more than just know God or love God; it gives us the tools to love like God as well."
Shane Stanford, author of *You Can't Do Everything . . . So Do Something*

IMMERSION
Bible Studies

COLOSSIANS,
1 & 2 THESSALONIANS

Lisa R. Withrow

Abingdon Press

Nashville

COLOSSIANS,
1 & 2 THESSALONIANS
IMMERSION BIBLE STUDIES
by Lisa R. Withrow

Copyright © 2011 by Abingdon Press

Library of Congress Cataloging-in-Publication Data

Withrow, Lisa R.
  Colossians, 1 & 2 Thessalonians / Lisa R. Withrow.
    p. cm. -- (Immersion Bible studies)
  ISBN 978-1-4267-1085-8 (curriculm--printed/text plus-cover, adhesive - perfect binding : alk. paper)
  1. Bible. N.T. Colossians--Textbooks. 2. Bible. N.T. Colossians--Criticism, interpretation, etc. 3. Bible. N.T. Thessalonians--Textbooks. 4. Bible. N.T. Thessalonians--Criticism, interpretation, etc. I. Title. II. Title: Colossians, 1 and 2 Thessalonians. III. Title: Colossians, First and Second Thessalonians.
  BS2715.55.W58 2011
  227'.06--dc22
                                2011005687

Editor: Stan Purdum
Leader Guide Writer: Stan Purdum

11 12 13 14 15 16 17 18 19 20—10 9 8 7 6 5 4 3 2 1

Manufactured in the United States of America

Contents

REVIEW TEAM

Diane Blum
Pastor
East End United Methodist Church
Nashville, Tennessee

Susan Cox
Pastor
McMurry United Methodist Church
Claycomo, Missouri

Margaret Ann Crain
Professor of Christian Education
Garrett-Evangelical Theological Seminary
Evanston, Illinois

Nan Duerling
Curriculum Writer and Editor
Cambridge, Maryland

Paul Escamilla
Pastor and Writer
St. John's United Methodist Church
Austin, Texas

James Hawkins
Pastor and Writer
Smyrna, Delaware

Andrew Johnson
Professor of New Testament
Nazarene Theological Seminary
Kansas City, Missouri

Snehlata Patel
Pastor
Woodrow United Methodist Church
Staten Island, New York

Emerson B. Powery
Professor of New Testament
Messiah College
Grantham, Pennsylvania

Clayton Smith
Pastoral Staff
Church of the Resurrection
Leawood, Kansas

Harold Washington
Professor of Hebrew Bible
Saint Paul School of Theology
Kansas City, Missouri

Carol Wehrheim
Curriculum Writer and Editor
Princeton, New Jersey

Immersion Bible Studies

A fresh new look at the Bible, from beginning to end,
and what it means in your life.

Welcome to IMMERSION!

We've asked some of the leading Bible scholars, teachers, and pastors to help us with a new kind of Bible study. IMMERSION remains true to Scripture but always asks, "Where are you in your life? What do you struggle with? What makes you rejoice?" Then it helps you read the Scriptures to discover their deep, abiding truths. IMMERSION is about God and God's Word, and it is also about you—not just your thoughts, but your feelings and your faith.

In each study you will prayerfully read the Scripture and reflect on it. Then you will engage it in three ways:

Claim Your Story

Through stories and questions, think about your life, with its struggles and joys.

Enter the Bible Story

Explore Scripture and consider what God is saying to you.

Live the Story

Reflect on what you have discovered, and put it into practice in your life.

IMMERSION makes use of an exciting new translation of Scripture, the Common English Bible (CEB). The CEB and IMMERSION BIBLE STUDIES will offer adults:

- the emotional expectation to find the love of God
- the rational expectation to find the knowledge of God
- reliable, genuine, and credible power to transform lives
- clarity of language

Whether you are using the Common English Bible or another translation, IMMERSION BIBLE STUDIES will offer a refreshing plunge into God's Word, your life, and your life with God.

1

Jesus Christ Is the Center

Colossians 1–2

Claim Your Story

I find it very easy to be distracted by special offers, sales, deals, and desires to buy something new to "make me feel good." I like change. I was born with a sense of adventure, and I have trouble with routine. So the discipline of keeping Christ at the center of my life on a daily basis when life is percolating along nicely challenges me; I have to work to keep a discipline.

On the other hand, I have friends who do not like change (though they do not mind shopping). It is more comforting to live with the "known" rather than the "unknown." However, they too may have a challenge when it comes to keeping Christ at the center, because doing so often yields change in our lives. If change is unwelcome, then avoiding it may mean avoiding an in-depth relationship with Christ.

Ultimately, no matter where we land in terms of our attitude toward change, keeping Christ at the center of life is hard. To do so requires intentional thought and practice every day, which is no easy feat.

Are you a person who welcomes change or avoids it? What blocks you from living a disciplined life that includes prayer and relationship-building with Christ? What might happen if you could center on Christ more fully? How might your life change? Would that change be life-giving or frightening? Why?

If you were to develop a spiritual discipline, who might you turn to for help when you feel tempted to neglect it? Would it be easier to maintain a discipline by having a person or a small group walking alongside you? Might Christian life flow within a group as well as through individual prayer?

The doxology sung in many churches begins with the words, "Praise God from whom all blessings flow." What does this "flow of blessings" mean to Christians when Christ is our center? Are they personal blessings? Do they encompass more than blessings for ourselves? If so, whom do they include?

As we read the letter to the Colossians, we hear encouragement for a life centered in Christ. This life yields blessings that carry us through difficulty and joy day-by-day.

Enter the Bible Story

Introduction and Background

Scholars who study Paul's writings disagree about whether he wrote Colossians or one of his disciples did. The uncertainty is because Colossians has an emphasis different from other writings that are indisputedly Paul's. For example, Paul writes in 1 Corinthians 15:20-24 about the tension between an only partly fulfilled realm of Christ in the present and the hoped-for, fully fulfilled future when Christ comes again. In contrast, Colossians focuses on transformation of the present by faith rather than emphasizing the future coming of Christ. Another difficulty in attributing this letter directly to Paul is that the words are presented in a celebratory way, in a poetic style rather than in Paul's usual confrontational manner.

So the question is whether Paul wrote this letter particularly for the Colossian and Laodicean Christians while he was in prison (where he might have changed his thinking), or whether a follower wrote in Pauline tradition, under Paul's name.

This practice of writing in a leader's name and using the leader's words was common in the era of the early church. We see this writer using Paul's typical benediction at the end of Colossians. We also see that this letter is similar in some ways to the letter to the Ephesians (written several decades later) in language and focus, indicating that the writer of Ephesians was familiar with the Colossian letter. Ultimately, we cannot be certain about the true authorship of this letter, though we know that it expresses Paul's concerns. However, for the sake of our study here, I will refer to the writer as Paul even though there are convincing arguments to the contrary, based on inconsistencies in style.

Colossians and Ephesians

Compare the following passages to see similarities, though not sameness, in these two letters, which likely means that they were dependent in style and content upon one another. In other words, the writer of one might have been familiar with the content and style of the other letter.
Colossians 1:1-2 with Ephesians 1:1-3
Colossians 1:23b-29 with Ephesians 3:7-9
Colossians 3:12-15 with Ephesians 4:2-4
Colossians 3:16-17 with Ephesians 5:19-20
Colossians 4:7-8 with Ephesians 6:21-22

Colossians appears to have been written in response to a controversy brewing in the church in Colossae (in Asia Minor) that has no direct parallel in the church today. Yet the letter invites us into a discussion that is as relevant and timely now as it was then. The immediate issue in the Colossian church was its exposure to a philosophy that claimed itself as a higher and purer form of Christianity, but which, says the writer of Colossians, "conform[s] to human traditions and the way the world thinks and acts rather than Christ" (2:8). The topic connects for us in that the writer pushes for focus on the centrality of Christ in an unfocused world that pulls people in competing directions. The question of centering on Christ rather than the lures of the world is the thread running through Colossians.

We do not know who was applying the pressure to believe the philosophy the letter opposes, but we do know that Paul was concerned for the well-being of the church as it began to veer in directions that seemed unfaithful to Christ's message. Paul and his followers wanted the young church to notice what mattered, what was meaningful about a Christ-centered faith and what fruits such a faith bears. This letter reminds them—and us—that meaning comes from living with Christ at our center no matter what our circumstances. Colossians provides us with a good picture of what Christ-centered living looks like in the midst of challenges and pressures.

Hymn to Christ

Without any information other than a letter and some historical fact-finding, it is difficult to understand exactly what question Paul was answering for the church in Colossae. We do know that the church founder and leader, Epaphras, was dealing with church conflict about Christian belief and practice there. The unsettled circumstances distracted members of the Colossae congregation from a focus on living in Christ. Paul wanted to support Epaphras as a leader in the congregation and did so by outlining right ways to think about faith and its meaning for life centered in Christ. In other words, the writer was calling for theological thinking or "doing" theology.

About the Christian Faith

Thinking Theologically

Theology is the study of God and how God works. We are thinking theologically when we focus on the nature and characteristics of God as we understand God in the world and in the universe. The New Testament letters use theological thinking as they work out faith questions. The letters answer questions or concerns presented by the early Christians who are considering what their faith means and who God in Christ is to them. Every Christian who takes faith seriously and asks questions about God, Christ, the Holy Spirit, and issues of the soul is a theological thinker.

The letter aimed to expose false teachings familiar in the ancient world. These teachings were creeping into the Colossian Christian community, and some viewed them as a supplement to the gospel Paul proclaimed. Paul, however, reminded the church that they were born through baptism into a particular tradition that was directly related to the apostles of Christ. To do so, he employed theological thinking to create arguments meant to keep people from going astray from Christ as the center of their lives.

The letter begins with a Pauline-like greeting to the saints, the faithful of the church (1:1-2). Usually, Paul's letters and those written in his name open with thanksgiving and prayer, like many church services do today. Colossians offers an especially lovely introduction because it includes a hymn to Christ (1:15-20). This hymn and a few concluding remarks urge the faithful to remember the meaning of their conversion, the nature and role of Christ, and the significance of their baptism (1:15-23). As you read the hymn, what do you find there that speaks to your understanding of Christ? of your baptism? Do its words address why you are a Christian?

Across the Testaments

Hymn to Christ

The writer of Colossians adapted the hymn in 1:15-20 to suit the purposes of the Colossian letter. Compare it to Proverbs 8:22-31 and note the similarities in content. Although the Colossian hymn refers specifically to Jesus the Christ rather than to Wisdom personified, there is a common theme in the two about existence before creation. Colossians 1:15-18a insists that Christ existed before creation, living as ruler of all creation including humankind and heading the church. Proverbs 8:22 says that God created Wisdom before creating the world. The Colossians hymn goes further, however; for in 1:18b-20, it indicates that Christ's reign is for all time, for all of creation, and his power is absolute.

The hymn itself directly confronts the misleading teachings about the power and worthiness of other gods. It places Christ squarely and exclusively at the center of all time, creation, and power. Stay steadfast! urges the letter. Christ has accomplished your salvation through his death and you are worthy to stand before God (1:22-23)!

Having appealed to the tradition into which the Colossians were baptized, the writer moves to another reason for staying faithful to the gospel they'd originally received: Paul's authority as an apostle of Christ, which validates his proclamation. In the past, God's message may have seemed a mystery to most people, secret to all but a few elite persons. But now Paul, having been given divine authority to reveal God's message, makes it plainly known to everyone. Paul asserts that Christ in each person is the hope of glory and wholeness of life (1:24-29). Christ at the center of life is the meaning of life and brings meaning to daily living.

Misleading Teachings

The writer expounds further on Paul's ongoing relationship with the congregation, though Paul is not with them. Paul wants the Colossian Christians to know of his concern to strengthen them in love and provide instruction in the wisdom and knowledge of Christ. The writer urges the Colossians not to listen to the words of false teachers (2:1-5) and to stay true to the faith Paul has revealed to them.

Now we get to the arguments against specific erroneous teachings that the Colossians have encountered. Refuting those teachings is the main purpose of the letter, and what better way to counter them than to claim Paul's authority and the divine tradition from which it comes? Christ has revealed truth to the Christians. By contrast, human theories come and go. Further, Christ alone is the fullness of God, the giver of salvation and the supreme authority. No other gods can make this claim. Only in Christ can Christians find full maturity and wholeness (2:6-10). Other teachings are theories that dabble in the latest trends and ideas.

The writer next expounds on the centrality and truth of Christ as opposed to other teachings by addressing baptism. The writer compares baptism to circumcision (2:11-12). Through circumcision, an individual shed the body of flesh and was initiated into God's covenant with Israel. Through baptism, the individual sheds the body of flesh and is initiated into Christ's church. Baptism brings the person into the realm of God and out of the realm where the forces of evil work.

Another way to put it is to view baptism as a burial and rising again with Christ (2:12), an act through which God forgives sins and makes the individual spiritually alive through Christ (2:13). Therefore, salvation comes from Christ, not from rituals or rules that are enslaving. Christ rules over all other cosmic beings and earthly beings because Christ is the way of salvation (2:14). The writer seems to chortle a bit after driving home the point, claiming that God will put false teachers in a parade of disgrace for all to see (2:15)!

The writer speaks of dying to the old life through baptism and rising to a transformed life while we live on this earth. Salvation occurs when we do this (2:12-13). We are forgiven, delivered from death-dealing ways, and given new life. It is then up to us to continue in the way of salvation, inviting the ongoing transformations that are available to us as we move closer to the mind and heart of Christ.

About the Scripture

Salvation

Some scholars define the term *salvation* as used in Christian theology as freedom from sin and death because of being in a right relationship with God through Christ; sin and spiritual death occur when one is disconnected from God. Others interpret the word to mean being saved from an afterlife, sometimes called hell, that continues to be an estrangement from God's love. In earlier biblical terms, *salvation* often meant rescue from actual slavery to rulers who occupied geographical territory. When the word *salvation* began to be used in spiritual terms, it shifted from rescue from physical slavery to freedom from the slavery of sin and subsequent spiritual death.

Intention and Practice

Christ becomes the center of our lives as we live as Christ would have us live, think as Christ would have us think, pray as Christ would have us pray—even for enemies' well-being. As we do so, we grow deeper in knowledge, perseverance, and faith. Strangely enough, the purpose for our lives becomes clearer when we focus on Christ at the center rather than the cries of the world to hitch on to the success wagon or the latest and greatest trend. To keep Christ at the center requires intention and practice.

The letter continues now with specific examples. The advocates of the erroneous philosophy were telling the Colossians to follow certain dietary laws, a sacred calendar, rituals, and life-practices as the means to salvation. In other words, the church members were being invited to earn salvation in an elite group of the saved by following particular rules or seeing visions set out by the false teachers. "Nonsense!" claims our writer. Christ and Christ alone is the source of salvation (2:16-19).

For us in our time, it is easy to practice religion as a set of rules of right-living, accomplished only by the "pure" Christians, without infusing our actions with a spiritual life that is sustained in Christ's love and grace. Living in Christ's love bears fruit: growth in the knowledge of God, strength of patience and endurance, and joy in God's power (1:9-12). No one who desires salvation is to be excluded, and no works can "buy" salvation. It is through Christ that God's grace provides salvation.

As in the early church, we find today that there are many voices around us, enticing us into a life that others tell us will lead to success, prestige, or riches. A phenomenon that began in the United States and now has spread around the globe has been dubbed the "prosperity gospel." The warnings in Colossians could just as easily apply to the prosperity gospel as they did to the erroneous philosophy of its day. The prosperity gospel distorts Christian teachings, claiming that if we pray correctly, ask the right things of God, and live in accordance to the Scriptures, God will bless us with riches and success. To many people who are poor and hungry or who have lived hard lives in other ways, this distorted gospel sounds like good news indeed. The evidence that this technique works seems clear when the preacher promoting it lives in a multimillion dollar home. People want that life, or at least a life that is a little easier, a little less burdened. These preachers seem to know how to get it and entice others into their elite circles.

However, many people find that though they pray as directed, ask the "right" things of God, and live lives in accordance to the Scriptures, their circumstances do not change. "Pray harder!" the voices cry; "You must not be doing the right thing! God wants you to be rich and successful!" Eventually, for those who do not see these promised results, one of two things occurs: They either become disillusioned with Christianity or they see through the false teachings about rituals and success and try to find a faith that has more meaning than earthly rewards.

At the end of Chapter 2, the writer wonders why the Colossians are still bound to the worldly understanding of faith rather than to Christ. False religion, practices that are attempts to secure elite status before God, and public displays of prayer all are signs of self-indulgence.

So we learn in the first two chapters of Colossians what it means to remain steadfast in faith even when external pressures push us to live more centered on the world than on Christ. The writer claims that one cannot live this way and be faithful to Christ. What is required of us is that we are intentional about centering on Christ from whom all blessings flow.

Live the Story

The letter to the Colossians encourages us to keep Christ at the center of our lives. Christ died; and in that death, Christ brought us salvation and new life. This good news calls us to focus on what Christ means for us and how our life flows from Christ in the center.

What barriers keep Christ from being at the center of your life? How do these barriers stay in place? What might it take in terms of prayer and community support to address these barriers? What life-changes are you willing to make to address them?

What does *new life* mean for you? What will new life in Christ lead you to do differently? How might you invite others into new life? How would you describe the meaning of life with Christ at the center? What matters most based on what you have learned in the letter to the Colossians? What are your blessings flowing from Christ?

Christ at the Center Guides Our Actions

Colossians 3–4

Claim Your Story

I am usually uncomfortable with personal conflict, especially when another person is raging at me. But my thinking about conflict changed when a friend suggested that the aggressor's actions might say more about that person than about me. That perspective helped me stop being so threatened and listen for what was causing the person discomfort or pain. To this day, anger and challenge still draw me up short; but after years of practice, I can ask myself, "What does this person need?"

All of us experience discord, sometimes even in the Christian community. Colossians reminds us that even though we may claim Christ, we sometimes find ourselves claiming things that are not of Christ as well. It's human nature to do so.

Imagine yourself managing a disagreement about the future of a group or of a congregation itself. You are trying to help folks find a way forward. But people are angry at each other; some want things to stay the way they have always been because the traditions are so meaningful while others want change in hope of bringing new life to the community. You notice that division occurs along age, gender, and in one case, family lines. You are aware that the conflict is escalating and people are beginning to displace their anger onto you. You ask, "What would Jesus do?" But the answer does not seem obvious.

How do you function in conflicted situations, when people are choosing sides? How do you treat them? How do you make decisions and help them make decisions? Are the answers to these questions what you want them to be?

What do you understand the Christian community to be? What is its purpose for the future? What is Christ doing in the world that calls for the church's help? What pain in the church community needs attention? What are you learning about people as they function in conflict?

The writer of Colossians does some theological work with the church in Colossae about these kinds of questions. Reliance on Christ's work in us and on the instruction found in this letter provide a way forward through difficult times, even those that leave us feeling like we live in disequilibrium.

Enter the Bible Story

In the first two chapters of the letter to the Colossians, Christians are encouraged to remember their baptismal vows and to stand steadfast against dangerous teachings that might cause them to veer away from true faith. Paul, or the person writing in Paul's name, counters the Colossians' temptation to worship pagan gods by reminding them that Christ is the ruler of the universe. The letter expresses concern about influences of false teachings on the congregation.

When we move to Chapters 3 and 4, there is a change in tone, moving toward a positive focus on Christian living. The next step for the Colossian congregation is to focus on Christ at the center of life, guiding transformed believers into a new way of living altogether.

Until Christ Comes

Colossians 3 and 4 encourage Christians to live a holy, Christ-centered life, filled with thanksgiving and meaning. Having already urged the

Colossians to remember their baptismal commitment and to resist false teachings, the writer now speaks of what a transformed life looks like. This orientation toward the realm of Christ rather than any false god or idol frees Christians from misleading teaching and from sin. According to Pauline theology, Christ rules all creation, and Christian inheritance comes to believers when Christ appears again (3:1-4).

Until Christ does come, Christians are to stay on moral ground, turn away from worldly orientation, and avoid God's judgment by shunning wrongdoing. In other words, even though Christ has already done the saving work that frees people from sin and death, personal and communal actions still matter.

Verse 5 implies that the new life in Christ requires some significant effort—so significant that the writer describes it as killing off parts of one's self: "So put to death the parts of your life that belong to the earth," the verse says and goes on to list some specifics, such as moral corruption and greed. The point is that new life requires ongoing development, which is hard work. The assumption, however, is that no one does this work alone because the whole community has its purpose focused on Christ. Therefore, all can encourage one another in the freedom of life in Christ, which requires intentionality every day. Without community encouragement, living an upright life is difficult indeed.

About the Scripture

The Fives

The writer of Colossians seems to like fives. Colossians 3:5 lists five characteristics of the worldly life, 3:8 states five characteristics of disobedience, and 3:12 counters the first two lists with five characteristics of the new life in Christ:
- Five worldly characteristics: sexual immorality, moral corruption, lust, evil desire, greed (idolatry)
- Five characteristics of disobedience: anger, rage, malice, slander, obscene language
- Five Christlike characteristics: compassion, kindness, humility, gentleness, patience

The Clothing Metaphor

To make his point about the change needed, Paul uses a clothing metaphor, encouraging Christians to "take off the old human nature" that sins and "put on the new nature" that imitates Christ's image (3:9-10). This life in Christ is available to everyone and does not discriminate against anyone. It welcomes all. Distinctions such as race, ethnicity, socioeconomic status, and nationality are rendered meaningless in Christ, according to Paul's teaching in Galatians 3:27-29 and in Philemon 15-19 as well as in verse 11 here. In God's eyes, each believer's status is equal. Of course, social status does not necessarily change for believers in Paul's times, but social status has no bearing on who can receive God's grace. Paul and his followers never intended to promote social status change; they were interested in communicating the good news of Christ to everyone who would listen.

So the good news is that everyone is welcome to new life in Christ. More difficult is the human response to God's grace that requires shedding sin and putting on virtuous living. This work of the Holy Spirit, which the writer does not mention here, is called *sanctification*.

Sanctification means that God is at work in us, and we participate in this work. What is it that we do? What does God do that brings new life and how do we respond? The writer does not give specifics, but provides some clues, including the clothing metaphor. When we put on a particular piece of clothing, we have a certain intention for it. For example, when we put on a sweater, we intend it to warm us. When we put on a pair of shorts, we may intend them to cool us down in hot weather. When we "put on" the characteristics that the writer lists in 3:12-14—compassion, kindness, humility, gentleness, patience, tolerance, forgiveness, and love— we have an intention for those characteristics, and we also see the outcome. When we wear compassion, it leads to action on behalf of others. When we wear patience, we allow events to unfold in surprising ways that we might have cut off if we were impatient. When we wear humility, we find that others may trust us as to act authentically and justly, to get ourselves out of the way so that we can focus on others. And so on.

About the Christian Faith

Sanctification

Sanctification occurs after we receive God's grace of *salvation*. God desires salvation for us and wants us to be in a human-divine relationship continually. To sanctify, or to make holy, one must contribute to the ongoing transformation of heart and mind with Christ at the center. God and human beings work together so that we can learn how to love each other, forgive each other, and live life counter to the world's values.

Christians are called to obey God and live in a way that brings praise to God's name. In this chosen state, Christians have the responsibility to live rightly for their own sake and for the sake of others, to walk in the way of sanctification. The Christlike qualities listed in 3:12-14 have bearing on how Christians witness to their faith in light of relationships with others. All of these qualities lead to actions based in love, shown through respect and care, for each other and for the stranger.

According to the letter to the Colossians, love is the highest mark of life in Christ, "the perfect bond of unity" (3:14). Meaning and purpose are found in the act of "putting on love," which promotes wholeness in the community and in the cosmos. Love leads to peace, which is the reconciliation of all things and peoples. *Peace* for Paul means depth and authenticity of commitment to Christ, resulting in wholeness rather than merely a personal feeling. In response to the love and peace found in Christ, Christians are to be thankful publicly in worship and in daily living (3:15-16). It is difficult *not* to be thankful when one experiences the peace of Christ, based in Christ's love!

The "Clothes" of Christian Living

When people live in Christ, they can live with thanksgiving, living in thankful community that holds itself together through singing (3:16; see also the hymn in Colossians 1:15-20) and praying. Early Christian communities were singers, with access to hymns and spiritual songs as well as the Psalms. One element of giving thanks in worship was through singing praises to God. It was not uncommon to have composers write songs specifically for congregational worship. Together, they prayed for help in obeying the call of Christ. These characteristics of Christian living made Christian communities unique in the first century and indeed, when practiced, continue to make Christians unique today. So, love, peace, virtue, and thanksgiving all result from a new life in Christ bestowed by God's grace (3:14-17).

What would political races look like today if these characteristics were practiced not only by politicians but also by the public? Would public discourse be more civil and more productive? Would social change be more acceptable? Would we call more people "neighbor" and even act more as a neighbor to others? These questions are implied in the text, where Colossians live with Christ in the center of their lives and in the center of their faith community and then go into the world to live in a Christian manner.

Christ makes no distinction based on race, class, or other humanly imposed categories (3:11). We are free in Christ *not* to be boxed into the social norms of our society. We are free in Christ *not* to have to defend ourselves every time someone pushes against us. We are free in Christ *not* to have to be the winner, *not* to have to be the one who is right all the time, *not* to have to be accumulating points for our success, *not* to have to exploit other people for our own desires. The world tells us that these getting-ahead actions are good for us, but Colossians tells us otherwise.

So when we face the conflicts that come our way, we do not need to be captured by them in ways that turn us toward worldly competition. Whether conflicts are personal or community-wide, political or in the business world, we can step back and remember whose we are and how Christ at our center leads us to acts of loving-kindness even in the midst of strife.

It does not take a huge leap of imagination to see how else the writer's advice might apply to us today. It would be interesting to discuss what the world might look like if a movement of Christians led the way in communicating, with the love and peace of Christ in mind and heart, about the unacceptable state of the world. We put on the clothes of Christian living!

Household Codes

At 3:18, there is a shift in topic, moving from the call to live in love and thanksgiving to the matter of household codes for Christians. These codes emphasize mutual respect that is characteristic of love-based ethical living. They may have been added here as examples of the writer's point or in response to a particular question posed to Paul. The codes or social norms of the time appear not only here in Colossians, but also in Ephesians 5:21–6:9, Titus 2:1-10, and 1 Peter 2:13–3:12.

Because there is little that is uniquely Christian in these codes, scholars believe they may have been taken from the social norms of the day and "Christianized" to fit the issues of ethical living at hand. It would be a mistake to quote the specifics of Colossians 3:18–4:1 as norms for American society today. Our context provides women with citizenship and the right to vote, job opportunities, right to inheritance, and potential roles either in addition to or, in some cases, instead of mothering and housekeeping. Children are considered fully human and capable of making simple decisions at a young age. Slavery is outlawed in the United States (though it still exists in illegal, underground forms), and so the admonishment to obey masters does not make sense to us in the way it did for first-century Colossian households. Nonetheless, while the household codes don't fit our lives today, the principle behind them does. And that principle is that all persons are equal in the eyes of Christ as spiritual beings and therefore, mutual respect must be observed for all people, no matter what their roles.

Across the Testaments

Household Codes

The codes or social norms of the time are listed in Colossians 3:18–4:1 briefly, but also in Ephesians 5:21–6:9, Titus 2:1-10, and 1 Peter 2:13–3:12. They speak of fairness and no partiality before God, a belief grounded in Jewish traditional sayings about God found in Deuteronomy 10:17, Job 34:19, and Psalm 82:1-4.

Practical Advice and Greeting

Verses 2-6 in Chapter 4 encourage the Colossians to be in watchful, thankful, and expectant prayer and to include Paul and his coworkers in their prayers. This section reminds the Colossian Christians to give attention to their moral life. When dealing with persons outside the church, Christians are to bear witness to their faith discreetly while being ready to respond to challenges others might bring to them. They must use appropriate language and display a gracious attitude when responding to each challenging situation. This practical advice echoes again the importance of keeping love and peace at the heart of communication, resulting from Christ-centered living.

The letter to the Colossians ends with personal information and greetings. Tychicus is the bearer of the letter to the young church and Onesimus accompanies him (4:7-9). Tychicus was also associated with Paul on a mission to Ephesus (see Acts 20:4 and 2 Timothy 4:12). Onesimus is the slave about whom the epistle to Philemon is written; Onesimus may be a Colossian himself traveling back to his master. Whether that is the case or not, Onesimus holds equal spiritual status to all others as a Christian.

The final section of the letter includes greetings to the Colossians on behalf of Paul and his associates and requests that greetings be sent to two sister churches: the one in Laodicea and the one that meets in the home of Nympha (4:15). In verse 14, Luke, the writer of the Gospel of Luke and of Acts, is called a physician for the first and only time in the New Testament.

After the Colossians have read this letter, they are to send it on to Laodicea for reading there. As was the custom in those days, letters were circulated among Christian communities for public reading. Likewise, the Colossians are also to receive and read the apostolic letter that was sent to the Laodicean church (4:16). Finally, the stenographer hands over the letter to Paul for a last benediction, bestowing grace upon the Colossians from his prison cell (4:18).

This letter reminds us that God's grace comes to us through Christ, who brings us salvation. We also are reminded that a response is required of us, namely that we participate in the ongoing work of becoming more holy (sanctifying work). To do so, we take on the mind and heart of Christ and live with these at our center as we interact in the world. The fruits of this intention show in our actions every single day.

Live the Story

It is encouraging that the writer of Colossians talks about freedom and equality in Christ. To find freedom and equality, we are urged to "take off the old nature" and "put on the new nature." That metaphor tells us that we can contribute to our ongoing growth as followers of Jesus.

What "garment of your old nature" do you need to remove from your wardrobe? How might you do so? What difference might that make in your home? in your church? in your life in the world? How will its removal affect your thoughts and actions?

What might make you reluctant to remove a particular part of your old nature? Are there persons in the church who can help you make the decision and hold you accountable?

What "new nature" do you need to intentionally "put on" in your daily life? What difference is that likely to make in the places you frequent? What freedoms might this new nature bring? How can God and the community help you in this process of change?

3

Living God's Message

1 Thessalonians 1:1–2:16

Claim Your Story

Have you ever been challenged because of your faith? Perhaps someone who is not a Christian or who is disillusioned with the church has questioned you. Or perhaps someone you know cannot understand why anyone would believe in God when the world seems so filled with tragedy and corruption. You may wonder the same things at times.

It seems that faith challenges are the order of the day in our society. Claims against Muslims, Jews, Christians, and pagans make the news frequently. Christianity is the dominant, most influential religion in the United States, as exhibited by the language we use and the assumptions we make in politics and social-action agendas. The Constitution claims that the United States is a land where freedom of religion is practiced; so in theory, all religions are welcome here.

Have you ever challenged someone else's faith or lack thereof? What made you wonder about that person's position? What did you say to or ask of the person? What did you think about that person's response? What did you feel?

What do you or would you say to someone who challenges your faith, who wants evidence from you for the presence of God? Can you create an argument or point to an experience that makes your faith clear? If so, what would that argument or experience be?

Have you ever felt persecuted for your faith? How do you keep your faith strong in the midst of these challenges?

Our U.S. context is almost the opposite of Paul's, where Christianity was a tiny movement, not well-received in most places, and even viewed with suspicion as a dangerous teaching. In some cities of the Roman Empire, Christians were persecuted. As we enter the Bible story, we will find that Paul's advice for the Thessalonians, who have to tread carefully in a world that does not trust them, includes reliance on the Holy Spirit to keep their own spirits strong.

Enter the Bible Story

Introduction and Background

First Thessalonians is considered the earliest written "book" in the New Testament. Paul wrote it from Corinth in the year 50 or 51, before the Gospels were written. Thessalonica, the capital of the Roman province of Macedonia (Greece), is where Paul, Timothy, and Silas (also known as Silvanus) founded a new church after Paul finished preaching in Philippi, ninety-five miles away (Acts 17:1-3). It is noteworthy that some of the converts were prominent Macedonian women, thought to be supporters of Paul's mission (verse 4). However, Paul was not able to spend much time in Thessalonica aiding the new church community in its faith and development.

Shortly after the church began to gather, opposition arose to Paul's message. He, Timothy, and Silas were accused by city officials of preaching obedience to a king other than Caesar (Acts 17:5-9); and they needed to leave quickly and quietly by night. Paul eventually went to Athens. Timothy and Silas stayed in nearby Beroea for a time before they rejoined Paul (17:13-15). Eventually, Paul sent Timothy back to Thessalonica to work with the Christian congregation there. Once Timothy returned to report to Paul, who by then had moved on to Corinth, Paul wrote this letter (1 Thessalonians 3:1-6).

First Thessalonians is divided into two parts. Chapters 1–3 address Paul's work in Thessalonica before he had to leave quickly without hope of return in the near future. He spends time in the letter talking about his mission, attempting to convince the new Christians that he is not another false prophet. Chapters 4–5 focus on the issues that the church is facing at the time of Timothy's second visit, including problematic actions of the congregation itself. Through this letter, we learn some of what an early Christian congregation looked like.

End Times

Near the end of the letter, Paul discusses the second coming of Christ and the end times. This emphasis on end times is called *eschatology*. Eschatology concerns all human beings, not just Christians. For example, today there are those who think about "end times" as what it would be like for human beings to destroy the environment and therefore, eliminate humanity altogether. Paul, though, addresses specifically *Christian* eschatology in response to a question some Thessalonians ask about the death of their Christian peers, wondering if anyone would be excluded from resurrection (4:13). Paul responds that the gathering up of the dead will occur in the end times. To make his point, he uses imagery that is called *apocalyptic*, meaning that the progress, timing, and events of end times are unveiled by God, usually in visions or vivid images, to a special messenger for the sake of the faithful. Not all understandings of end times

---

About the Christian Faith

Eschatology and Apocalyptic Style

Eschatology is the study of the end times, meaning the end of the world or the end of humankind. Many religions and some scientists think eschatologically (about the end of the world). The *eschaton*, a Greek word, is the "end," or in Christian thinking, the divinely ordained climax of history. *Apocalyptic narrative* or *apocalyptic style* as found in the book of the Revelation of John is prophecy or revelation in vivid imagery about the eschaton, the end times, usually told in terms of great destruction or devastation. So *apocalyptic imagery* is one way to symbolize what the *eschaton* might look like.

are apocalyptic, but this tradition of describing God's revelation was a feature of late Hebrew Scripture and early New Testament times.

Think for a moment what you have heard about the end times. How do movies and books describe these times? Are the descriptions apocalyptic, involving mass destruction? Apocalyptic imagery remains common today in both secular and religious circles, partly because the drama attracts people and partly because we have little understanding of end times and what they might look like. One common Jewish understanding of end times was "the end of an era," usually the fall of a political-religious reign, described in vivid imagery and metaphor. Christians today who accept the more popular understanding of a final, overarching apocalypse, or a mass destruction of the world at the end times, tend to want God to bring about violent justice to all the earth based on Christian values and truth-claims. Media creators use graphic imagery today to portray the end times in a similar way to how the speakers and writers of Paul's time used images that were familiar in their contexts.

Paul himself thought that the end times were very near and that he would see them in his lifetime. It did not turn out that way, and eventually, he had to revise his thinking. Early Christians were told to watch for Christ's coming, and thus many were convinced that a cataclysmic shift would occur soon. Some people began to lose heart as time passed; so later, Paul and his followers found it necessary to reassure Christians about maintaining faith. Second Thessalonians is one example of this.

Across the Testaments

Old and New Testament References to the End Times

Apocalyptic eschatology, or vivid imagery describing a revealed time and place for the end times, can be found in both testaments. For example, the writer of Daniel uses this imagery (see Daniel 7–8). Other places where this approach to unveiling the nature of the end times can be found are in Second Thessalonians, Mark 13 (and its parallels in Matthew and Luke), Second Peter, and Revelation.

The belief in a specific end time assumes that God has a particular plan that stops the world's increasing sin and spiritual disconnection by intervening and making all things right. Early Christians believed that Jesus' resurrection was the beginning of the end times; soon Christ would return as the final judge of the world.

What is your understanding of the end times? Is there an end time in sight? What would it look like? Does the idea of end times being part of a significant shift in political and spiritual power make sense, or are the end times meant to be for all the earth's destruction and the final victory of God? What about all the people who claim a date for the end of the world based on prophecy; how are they convinced about those dates?

Thanksgiving and the Holy Spirit

Paul's letters always begin with general thanksgiving for the life of the church and its people. He begins this letter with acknowledgment and gratitude for the faith, love, and hope exhibited by the church in Thessalonica. Paul notes that work is a form of faith, that effort is the way of love, and that perseverance or steadfastness is the way to show hope (1:3). Paul affirms in his letter that God chose the Thessalonian Christians through God's own loving initiative to be in divine-human relationship together. Paul observed evidence of the Holy Spirit's presence among the Thessalonians when he was present among them, preaching his message of the good news of Christ. The Thessalonians received the message powerfully and "with deep conviction" (1:5a). The Spirit was at work as Paul preached, resulting in effort and faithful perseverance in the Thessalonians, for which Paul gives thanks (1:2, 6-7).

The power of the Holy Spirit is apparent to people who worship in the Pentecostal and charismatic traditions today, no matter what their denomination. Reliance on the work of the Spirit is their very foundation of life in Christ. Those who rely less intentionally on the movement of the Holy Spirit may use different language to describe transformative change or startling events in their lives. I hear the words "It's a God-thing!" quite

About the Christian Faith

The Holy Spirit

The notion of the Trinity—God, Christ, and Holy Spirit—as three Persons in one, had not been fully developed in Paul's day, though mention of the Holy Spirit can be found in the Gospels and New Testament letters. Paul has a sense of the movement of God's Spirit in young churches he established, noting that conversions occurred during preaching or conversation. Baptisms occurred in the name of God, Christ, and the Holy Spirit; so there is a movement toward an understanding of Trinity. However, when we speak of the Trinity, we are speaking of a doctrine that was established in the year 325 at the Nicene Council. In the biblical writings, we see the roots for this doctrine.

often when someone is trying to explain an event or feeling that does not make logical sense otherwise.

One way we encounter the work of the Holy Spirit is when we receive a word or feeling that meets our need. For example, some people who experience shock or grief also subsequently find a seemingly inexplicable peace that fills their very beings. Or someone who does not know what to do with the future waits and watches, and often the path becomes surprisingly clear. Sometimes people have trouble letting go of anger or resentment, but then there is a sudden release that brings freedom.

Imagine what word you need today from the Spirit. What happens when you receive the Holy Spirit's presence? What do you do? What do you say? Notice how the Holy Spirit moves in others, not necessarily in worship, but throughout your day. What happens? What do they do? What do they say? Do they know that the Holy Spirit is moving in them? Paul mentions that he sees results from the Holy Spirit's work in the Thessalonians as imitators of Paul and his followers (1:3-6). Do these results make sense? Are there other results? What are the fruits of the Spirit?

As we move forward in the letter, we notice that Paul gets more specific about the conversions occurring in Thessalonica. As he himself attempts to live with transparency so that the Holy Spirit can work through him, he rejoices in the new Christians who imitate him and then become models for others to imitate. The message and the person of Paul are inseparable, unlike other religious preachers who "sell" a message that differs from how they live. Paul is pleased that this holistic way of being faithful through living the good news as well as speaking it is also evident in the Thessalonian Christians (1:6-8).

At this point, it would be helpful to reflect on who we imitate in our lives and why, but it's equally helpful to turn the thought around: Who imitates us? Why? What do they see and what would we want them to see? Are there characteristics of Paul that we would want to imitate or that we show to others?

Sources of Christianity

Chapter 1 concludes with a thanksgiving for turning from idols (worship of many gods, called *polytheism*), to the one true God (*monotheism*) (1:9-10). Monotheism, worshiping one God, was a core principle for the Jews. In fact, what set the Jews apart thousands of years before the birth of Jesus, and eventually set Christians apart as well, was their belief in one God, rather than many gods. Jews and Christians in the early Christian era were still surrounded by people who believed in many gods, each with different powers and tasks. Later, Islam also emerged as a monotheistic faith.

Studies of Greek and Roman mythology name gods and goddesses and the supposed powers each held. When Paul refers to idols, he likely is referring to all gods that are not the one God, calling the Gentiles to give up their pagan beliefs for the truth of one God, revealed in Christ. (*Pagan* today usually refers to one who is not a Christian, Jew, or Muslim, but is polytheistic in belief; but it is also sometimes used to refer to someone who has no religion at all.)

The early Christians, drawing on Jewish tradition initially, added the message of Jesus and the Resurrection with emphasis on Christ's second coming. They also emphasized the connection with Jesus as Christ, the one who delivers Christians from sin and death. Notice that Paul does not specifically mention the things Jesus taught during his time on earth. The emphasis instead is on Jesus as the Christ, Savior of the world. Paul focuses on working out the meaning of faith rather than the meaning of Jesus' specific teachings, which are made known later when the Gospels are written. It may be that Paul was less familiar with stories about Jesus' work than with Jesus' status as the Son of God. Paul would have heard about Jesus' death and resurrection as the salvation of the world, which matters more to Paul than Jesus' life on earth.

God at Work in Thessalonica

We begin the second chapter by reading additional reassurances that the word of God is being spoken through Paul rather than Paul speaking his own, human word. He repeats that the evidence of God's transformational word is among the people of the Thessalonian church, found in their changed lives. Paul prays that this word continues to transform them so that they may grow in holiness (sanctification).

We find a jarring interruption in 2:14b-16. Suddenly, Paul seems to be attacking the Jews as responsible for killing Jesus and driving out the Jesus-followers from Jerusalem. What troubles some scholars about this passage is that it does not fit with Paul's usual attitude toward the Jewish people.

Biblical scholars debate whether Paul suddenly has a temper tantrum in the middle of his letter or if this section was added by someone else after Paul's death, spurred by the destruction of Jerusalem by Rome in A.D. 70. Some people interpreted that disaster as God's wrath against the Jews. Anonymous later additions to written materials were common in the New Testament era. Whatever the case, this passage has been and still can be dangerously destructive, especially when used to justify anti-Semitic sentiment in our own contexts. Such use of the text is not appropriate, particularly in light of Paul's call to act in love. What's more, in Romans 9–11, Paul defends the Jewish heritage and confirms that the Jews are special in God's sight. Having said that, we note that 1 Thessalonians 2:14b draws a parallel between the persecution of Thessalonian Christians and the persecution of Jewish-Christians in Judea.

As Paul gives thanks for the Thessalonians and encourages them to persevere in the faith despite opposition, he reinforces their understanding of the transforming power of the Holy Spirit in their lives. Even though Paul is separated from the church in Thessalonica, he celebrates their conversions and their work. It is clear in this letter that Paul has personal affection for the Christians in Thessalonica.

Live the Story

Paul counsels reliance on the Holy Spirit. He rejoices in the evidence that conversions were taking place when he visited the Thessalonians. But the Holy Spirit does not stop with conversion; the Spirit has the power to sustain us in the challenges we face and to provide solace for others.

Can you name the times when you have seen the Holy Spirit at work recently? What does the Holy Spirit do in order to get your attention? Or does the Spirit continue to move and leave it to each person to choose whether or not to connect with the movement? How have you seen the Holy Spirit move in someone else? in a particular situation? What helped you identify that movement as being from God?

How might you be present to others, embodying God's message for those who suffer—at work, at home, in the extended family, in the world? What might be shown to the teenagers who need a word of hope when they experience bullying or depression? What might be the Spirit's work through you for hyper-busy friends or family? How might Christ's presence be made known to someone who cannot leave the house? How does the movement of the Holy Spirit differ from simply wanting to help other people?

What blessings does the Holy Spirit bring to you? to others? to the church? to the world?

4

Travelers Who Accompany Us Enliven Our Faith

1 Thessalonians 2:17–3:13

Claim Your Story

An African proverb says, "I am because we are." It implies that no one can be fully human without community. Likewise, no community is possible without individuals gathered together. One important function of a faith community is to build each other up in belief and practice.

Scientific studies show that long periods of isolation tend to breed chemical changes in our brains, sometimes leading to mental disorders. By correlation, long periods of isolation from our spiritual community can lead to soul disorders. In Paul's time, community was necessary to build up the faith because Christians were persecuted and needed support. In our country today, we Christians have freedom and may feel less need for spiritual community, while in fact, we need community more than ever.

Have you been without a spiritual community for any extended period? What was that like? If you are in such a community now, what difference does it make to your soul? Is there a sense of hope about the future in the community?

Think for a moment about those persons who have made a difference in your life of faith. What are they like? What do they do? How do they conduct themselves? How do they understand hope? Have they enlivened your faith? How? What do they mean to you?

Now think about how you have made a difference in the faith journeys of others. How did you do it? Was this impact on their lives intentional? What happened? How did you conduct yourself? How do you understand hope?

Imagine what it would be like to live on the proverbial deserted island for one year with no other living human being or creature, no means of communication, and no entertainment. Even if your basic needs were supplied, what would happen to you physically, spiritually, and emotionally? Would you suffer? How would you keep hope alive?

Paul spends time in First Thessalonians emphasizing the need for community, especially when the early Christians found themselves in a hostile environment. He continues his letter with a message about perseverance and hope found in Christian community.

Enter the Bible Story

Worrying About Friends

In the seventeen verses we are considering in this session, Paul praises the faith and practice of the members of the church in Thessalonica. He has invested time and travel as well as spiritual and emotional energy in this group of people, and he is frustrated that he cannot be with them now. Paul wishes it were otherwise, but a letter will have to do at this point.

Nonetheless, Paul uses the letter to tell the Thessalonian Christians what a warm place they hold in his heart. He has already expressed his thanks for them (1:2) and for the way they welcomed the gospel message (2:13). He's aware that they know that he didn't run out on them, but was, in fact, forced to leave (Acts 17:5-10). But he now wants to make sure they understand that his *continued* absence from them is not by choice. There are likely a variety of reasons behind his statement in 1 Thessalonians 2:18, that "we wanted to come to you — I, Paul, tried over and over again — and Satan stopped us." They possibly include illness, matters in Corinth (from where he is writing) requiring his attention, his reputation with the city officials in Thessalonica as a troublemaker (Acts 17:8), and the hostility of certain Jews in Thessalonica who had even pursued him to the next town on his route (17:13).

Nonetheless, Paul assures the brothers and sisters of the church that he did not work for their conversion to abandon them to difficulty (probably persecution because of their Christian belief); at the coming of Christ, they will be his glory and joy (1 Thessalonians 2:19-20).

About the Christian Faith

Paul's References to Satan

Satan, or in the original Hebrew, *the satan*, is considered to be the accuser or adversary, subservient to God. In Paul's writings, Satan or the tempter is one who actively stands in the way of right-relationship with God. Second Corinthians 2:10-11 and 11:12-15 refer to Paul's understanding of the struggle between God and Satan as the oppositional force.

Over time, the understanding of Satan has evolved; different religious groups use different names for this oppositional force. In some Christian circles, ancient and modern, Satan is understood as a fallen angel, too proud to worship God as the other angels do. Even art has anthropomorphized Satan, giving this accuser and adversarial force a human look, sometimes with wings, sometimes with merely horns and a threatening tail. This personification of a force counter to God gives a name to the evils that occur in the world, the choices and decisions that people make to the detriment and sometimes destruction of others and, ultimately, themselves.

While Paul could not come personally, he had sent Timothy back to the Thessalonians to strengthen and encourage them in faith. Paul's mention of this now leads him to comment that suffering is often part of the Christian life—indeed, perhaps suffering is even a confirmation of true Christian faith. Paul reminds his readers that he had predicted that sufferings would come to them. By saying this, Paul is seeking to stabilize the community in light of suffering, knowing how tempting it can be to give up the faith under external pressure (3:3-4). Paul's concern about this issue was deep. When he couldn't "stand it anymore," he sent Timothy, who has now returned with a good report (3:5-6).

Perhaps you have suffered, are suffering, or know someone who is. While with the Thessalonians Paul was probably referring to persecution because of their identity as Christians, some people also see all suffering—physical and otherwise—that comes to Christians as ways in which God teaches lessons of endurance. Others do not agree, but understand that God is with them in their suffering. Still others see no reason for suffering and do not understand why circumstances lead to suffering. Where do you stand?

As mentioned, Paul's emphasis on suffering as part of the Christian life refers to the persecution that Thessalonian Christians are experiencing because of their newfound beliefs. Suffering confirms faith because this faith is challenging pagan and Jewish belief systems in ways that make others uncomfortable. Its newness, its reliance on Christ, sounds either ridiculous or dangerous to outsiders, a common response when new religions enter arenas where people have not heard of them before.

Across the Testaments

Suffering

A great number of biblical writings attempt to address people's relationship with God in the midst of suffering. Isaiah 53 is commonly used to describe suffering in light of serving God, showing some parallels to how Christ later suffered, as an innocent person afflicted for the sake of God's message to the world. The early Christians connected with this affliction when they too suffered because of their beliefs and service to God.

Facing Challenges to Faith Today

Those who accompany us with love on the faith journey not only support us in suffering, but also create spaces for us to become more centered in Christ and more truly who we are. These people are the ones I call living saints because they are invested in my wholeness and the state of my soul. Their proddings and questions help my faith mature in vital, life-giving ways. They are people who bring me hope and renewal.

Ironically, sometimes opposition helps strengthen our faith. I know that when I have to defend what I believe, I learn how to articulate what matters and how to stake a claim for my faith. Likewise, in ongoing interfaith conversations occurring around the world, there is growing commitment to welcoming diverse understandings of God, without giving up our own understanding. Representatives from different faith backgrounds learn to articulate why they believe what they do in light of the questions from others who are trying to understand significant differences. Theological debate sharpens our focus and stance.

Being able to speak about our faith is important today, even in the U.S. where a growing number of people are skeptical about Christians. Admittedly, these skeptics sometimes base their conclusions about Christianity in general on a few people who claim to be acting in Christ's name, who make their way into the news because of some intolerant statement or threatening act. Those who claim to be Christians and who blow up buildings or threaten others' lives, attempt to rewrite history in their favor, burn books, or declare war on other faiths, get a great deal of attention. Christians who quietly get on with life either receive little attention or are assumed to be much like those in the media. In many ways, Christianity has garnered a bad name in this country. That's why the phrase "I'm spiritual but not religious" arises in so many conversations. Many Americans do not want to have anything to do with organized religions. For example, in a 2009 survey by the research firm LifeWay Christian Resources, 72 percent of Millennials (18- to 29-year-olds) said they're "more spiritual than religious."[1] This claim is so common now that the acronym SBNR (spiritual but not religious) can be found on its own Web site, in Wikipedia, and on Facebook (SBNR.org).

This trend is not really a form of persecution, as in Paul's time, but it is an oppositional stance toward being in Christian community as a faith-supporting, accountable group of people. So Paul's urging the Thessalonians to remain steadfast in building up the faith and the faith community is relevant for us today. SBNR movements discount the importance of community in the development of spiritual wholeness through accountability and support. Paul is right in First Thessalonians when he emphasizes the need for community in the midst of those who are anti-Christian (in his case) and anti-church (in ours). When we do not function within the faithful community, we are subject to whims and desires without an anchor, and we find it much harder to remain steadfast on the journey.

Staying Connected

After Paul makes his point about staying steadfast despite suffering, he returns to Timothy's report (3:6). The Thessalonian faith-community is doing well in faithfulness and love and retains a high opinion of Paul, Timothy, and Silas. (Note that there is no mention of hope at this point; Paul deals with that a bit further on, as we will soon see.) Timothy's report has comforted Paul in his distress in Corinth. Paul emphasizes his personal involvement in the life of the young church by declaring his gladness that they are standing firm in difficult circumstances (3:8).

It is striking that Paul is so concerned about his relationship with this church. Perhaps that is because this church was one of the earliest he initiated. Whatever the reason, Paul is determined to remain personally connected with the Thessalonian congregation as it matures in Christ. He deeply regrets that he cannot visit at this time, but wishes to stay in touch as much as he can. From Timothy's report, it is clear that the church, too, would like Paul to visit them, for they have more questions about the faith than he has answered. However, the visit is not to be.

Imagine what it might be like to have just started a new Christian spirituality group, but then learn that you cannot be there beyond the initial start-up because your job requires you to move far away. You are the one who has developed the passion for the group's existence in the first place. You have experience with small groups. You know the information the participants need. You are the person to whom they turn when they have questions. But now, circumstances do not allow you to be there, so you have to resort to phone calls, online meetings, Facebook connections, or e-mail. What would you like them to know about your absence? How would you reassure them that you are not abandoning them? What would you like to know about them? Think about how you would act in Paul's situation. Would you do anything differently? If so, what would that be?

The Theme of Hope

The closing verses in Chapter 3 (3:9-13) are listed in the lectionary (the suggested Bible readings for worship set out in yearly cycles) for the first Sunday of Advent in some years. One reason for this Scripture selection is Paul's focus on hope, the most significant theme of Advent. In the season of waiting, we are asked to have patience and love as we look for the coming of Jesus, our hope. Paul's emphasis in this letter is on the hope of the Second Coming; but he, too, is waiting. So we see both in the Advent worship emphasis and in this text the parallel senses of waiting and hope for the blessing of Christ to come.

The themes connect in another way as well. How do we make ourselves ready as we wait during Advent? How do the Thessalonians prepare for the Second Coming as they wait? Ultimately, we see that Paul is calling for the church to be forward-looking while it moves forward in time. To be forward-looking means to be transforming the present as people change how they think and act in a life lived in hope. This message makes sense for the early church in particular, but it also makes sense for today's church, which at times has a tendency to be backward-looking. We are to nurture hope in Christ's presence among us—good news to share with the world—just as Paul encourages the early church to do.

A Benediction

Paul closes this first half of the letter with a prayer of blessing for God's love to surround the relationship between the Thessalonian congregation on the one hand and himself and his coworkers on the other (3:11-13). Paul still hopes to return to see the church soon. But whether present with them or yearning for them from afar, his prayer for them is that increasingly love for one another will continue to advance holiness and stability, enriching a faith that is grounded in God while they wait in hope for the Second Coming.

For three chapters, Paul has declared his love for the Thessalonians; now, in verse 12, he asks them to love each other as he loves them, and in turn, to love those who are beyond their own community.

In sum, this benediction, found in the middle of the full letter, finds Paul gathering together the points he has already made: his concern for the community staying steadfast in the faith, his relief at Timothy's positive report that they have done so, and his love for the Thessalonian Christians. He then foreshadows his own trajectory into the next part of the letter to address the blameless and holy living of the congregation (3:11-13).

It may seem odd to find a benediction in the middle of a letter, but there is a certain logic to its placement. In our worship services benedictions serve as transitions from one space to another. We move from our intentional worshiping community out into the world where we function in less ordered ways, reacting to the variety of events that come in our direction. The benediction here also signals a change. Paul's prayer carries the readers from the past, to the present when he uses the word "now" (3:11), to the future.

The first part of the letter celebrates the friendship of Paul with the new church. Paul writes supporting and encouraging words, concluding here with a desire for reunion with the Thessalonians and for their growth in love, which is necessary preparation for the coming of Christ. Paul then moves to the present desire to meet again. The future is addressed when Paul states what the next conversation is to be about, with his intent to help the Thessalonians increase their faith. We are about to move with Paul to the second half of the letter where he focuses on how these young Christians will live with each other and understand Paul's theology of death and resurrection.

The benediction signals movement. Think for a moment about your movement through your faith journey. How did the journey start? What were transition points? Where is the journey now? What have you learned over time? Who was involved? As Paul is companion to the Thessalonian church's journey, we too find companions on our way for our journeys.

Live the Story

In our current "spiritual but not religious" climate, articulation of a reasoned, yet vitally experienced faith is rare but important. Paul works hard to encourage the Thessalonians to be able to speak about their Christian life in ways that are understandable and helpful to others. He wants to make sure that they hang on to faith and hope in the midst of difficult times.

Paul also recognizes the power of the believing community to enliven one another's faith.

What about Christian community hinders faith development? What in the wider community/world hinders faith development? What hindrance to spiritual growth should the community rid itself of?

What about Christian community helps faith development? What in the wider community/world fosters faith development?

Does "faith community" simply mean local church? What is a wider understanding of faith community? How are connections made among various communities? How wide does the understanding of "community" go?

How would you speak about your faith to someone who says she or he is spiritual but not religious? What would you say about the importance of continual connection with a faith community? What have you learned in community that you might not have learned on your own? What does "I am because we are" mean to you as a Christian?

In light of what you've learned in this lesson, what actions might you take to help other worshipers grow in Christ?

[1] See John Blake, CNN Living. June 3, 2010, *http://articles.cnn.com/2010-0603/living/spiritual. but.not.religious_1_spiritual-community-religious-god?_s=PM:LIVING.*

5

Life Is Hard, But Hope Is Real

1 Thessalonians 4–5

Claim Your Story

Life is hard, and some personal problems seem unsolvable. Consequently, there are times when we run a bit short on hope. We may sink into despair and struggle to find a way out. Or we may simply endure difficult times and wait until they pass, praying that they do. Perhaps we search for new sources of hope, for new ways to think about our situations that differ from how we might have understood them previously.

One of the ways which the Christian community experiences hope is by listening to the good news of God's love presented over and over through Scriptures, through preaching and teaching, through conversation and witness. God's self-revelation to the world through Jesus tells us that God cares about our human condition and wants a relationship with us. That God would promise us life after death tells us that God wants to remain connected with us for all time.

Name ways that you may have felt hopeless in life. Did hope return? If so, how did that happen? What did the return of hope feel like or sound like in your mind? Did your perspective or language change? Now think about those who seem hopeless to you. What message would make sense to them? Is there a way to walk with them in their hopelessness that would bring them comfort? What can you tell them about your hope that might be meaningful to them?

Think about the hope-filled messages that you hear in church, in the community, or through your own studies and readings. What do these messages bring to your life? How has your understanding of hope changed over time? What do you do when there is more despair than hope around you? What are the most hopeful people you know like? How do they sustain hope?

Hope seems elusive in our world today. Unemployment, poverty, meanness, and violence are in the news all the time. When we do hear a message of hope, we feel some relief. Living as Christians means to live in hope. Paul knew this very thing when he set about to assure the Thessalonians about their relationship with God in life and in death. Paul's words to the Thessalonians in the last two chapters of the letter are intended to sustain hope.

Enter the Bible Story

Living a Holy Life

In Chapter 4, Paul calls the Thessalonian Christians to right living. He reminds them to live ethically, with actions and attitudes that please God. Remember, the Gospels were not written yet, so Paul had little of Jesus' teaching tradition from which to draw. He based his encouragement on what his conversion (Acts 9:15-20) taught him about the meaning of right relationship with God and on what he learned from other Christ-followers (for example, see Acts 9:26-30 and Acts 13).

God wants Christians to live their lives "dedicated to him" (1 Thessalonians 4:3) each day as a part of a lifelong process to achieve true holiness (sanctification). Paul gets specific about ethical living, targeting primarily sexual exploitation (4:3-7) and taking advantage of others (4:6) as two areas where humanity goes astray. In the Common English Bible (CEB), verse 6a refers to not taking advantage of others "in this issue,"

Across the Testaments

Old Testament Roots of Paul's Message to the Thessalonians

First Thessalonians 4:1-12, in which Paul discusses living in ways that please God, draws upon the understanding of ancient Hebrew laws laid out in Leviticus 17–26, revised for the context of the early Christian age.

Paul's discussion in 1 Thessalonians 5:1-7 about Christ's coming being an unpleasant surprise to those who are complacent echoes a theme found in the Old Testament as well (Jeremiah 6:14 and 8:11; Ezekiel 13:10; Micah 3:9-11). Leaders of the synagogues and rulers of countries claimed that God was on their side, when in fact, the prophets warned that one day, there would be a great and unexpected surprise leading to their destruction.

but the underlying Greek is a business term often translated as "in this *matter.*" A useful comparison is the New Revised Standard Version (NRSV), where 4:6a reads "that no one wrong or exploit a brother or sister in this matter." So, while Paul speaks to the Thessalonians about staying away from prostitutes and avoiding a variety of other sexual sins, he also urges honesty rather than greed in business.

Prostitution, often called the oldest profession, was common in biblical times. Men, women, and children could be bought for sex. Prostitution then, much like today, was a last-resort way to make enough money to finance basic needs when people were destitute. For example, widows who did not have an extended family to care for them were in great difficulty. They had no social welfare and were not allowed to participate in the job market—with the exception of commercial sex work. Paul was especially concerned about children in sex work. Some scholars believe that when he refers to sexual relations in his letters, he is specifically talking about prostitution. Paul is aware that the world around the Christian church tolerates varied, and sometimes abusive, sexual practices. He also knows that the church can never tolerate such things and still be the church.

Paul drives his point home: God is invested in and committed to our living ethically and therefore brings negative consequences for those who are not obedient to God's will (4:6b). He reminds his readers that these instructions do not come from him, but from God who gives the Holy Spirit to strengthen Christians in holy, right living as a means of sanctification (4:8).

Paul knows of the Thessalonians' loving deeds beyond their own community. It is clear in verses 9-12 that the church in Thessalonica has made contact with other young churches in the region. But Paul also addresses a problem, perhaps gossip and idleness exhibited by some of the community, by encouraging further and deeper attention to loving works toward others. He sounds, in verses 11-12, like a parent who wants the best for his children, encouraging them to get a job and mind their own business. What's more, he does not want Christians to be dependent on others for their keep. Paul himself made sure that he was gainfully employed everywhere he went, so that he would not have to rely on charity. He emphasizes work and attention to behavior because the behavior of Christians reflects on the church itself; Paul is concerned about the reputation of the church in a world that thinks it suspect in the first place.

What things in your faith community do not reflect well on the church? What does the outside world see regarding how members and attendees act? Is there gossip or in-fighting? What things might Paul be concerned about if he were to visit your church or community?

Picture what happens when a person of color, a person with a disability, or a white woman enters a white male-oriented business. The insiders watch the person who is "different" to see how he or she acts, dresses, and approaches work. The scrutiny is often higher for those who seem different than for someone who is similar to everyone else. Does this kind of response happen also in the church today? The connection is clear here: the early church is the "different" one in a Gentile, pagan society and therefore, it is watched very carefully. Paul wants to make sure that the church suffers no accusations because of poor or dishonest behavior by its members.

Death and Resurrection

In verse 13, Paul addresses a problem the Thessalonians themselves have raised. In light of Paul's teachings about Jesus' resurrection, they do not understand how death can occur for Christians at all and, therefore, are worried that only those who are alive at Jesus' return will be raised to join him in the final days. In other words, Christians are wondering why baptism into the death and resurrection of Christ has not made them immortal, avoiding death completely. Jesus had conquered death! They were hearing a confusing message from other teachers, that those who had died before Christ's coming had missed out on resurrection.

Certain rituals in various pagan cults were supposed to have granted immortality, so it seems natural for the Thessalonians to believe the same of baptism. Paul does not wish to deny grief over the loss of loved ones, but he is concerned about the people's despair about the dead not rising with Christ at Christ's second coming. So their question to Paul was a theological one: Who is included in rising with Jesus when he comes again? Are the ones who died already included? Are they really dead? Paul assures them that every Christian, both the dead and the living, will experience resurrection (4:14-15). In verse 14, Paul says that because Jesus died and rose, God also will bring all who "died in Jesus" to new life.

Verses 15-17 spell out details as Paul has worked them out thus far: At the time of Christ's second coming, the dead shall rise first. Then, together with Christians still alive, they will "meet with the Lord in the air" (4:17) where heaven and earth meet. (Note the use of apocalyptic imagery here, which Paul inherited from apocalyptic Jewish tradition.) According to Paul, Christ will descend from heaven with heaven's whole hierarchy of angels (verse 16), led by the head angel's shout and a blast on God's trumpet. In Paul's time, many believed that divine authority in heaven consisted of hierarchies of power, with various layers of angels having different ranks. In verse 16, Paul refers to the "head angel," who has the honor of sounding the trumpet calling on all the ranks of angels, as Christ descends to gather all of the living and the dead together at his coming again.

The end times (the *eschaton*) will include the resurrection of all believers, and it is clear that Paul expects to be alive at the second coming (*parousia* in Greek) of Christ. What happens to nonbelievers is never mentioned here, though there is room for speculation that Paul believes that

About the Scripture

Paul's Beliefs About End Times (*eschaton*)

First Thessalonians 4:15-17 does not give us a complete picture of Paul's full belief (theology) about the end times, and there is no conclusive belief statement from Paul regarding this matter. In fact, notions of the *eschaton* differ throughout the New Testament, indicating that many ideas were circulating in the early churches. For example, see the differences in Mark 13 and Revelation.

However, the point of discussion about the *eschaton* is not to establish a timeline or a series of events that can be expected to play out just as Paul describes. Instead, the purpose is to convey that God eventually will claim victory over oppositional forces through the saving work of Christ, establishing God's reign over all the universe.

all people will benefit from Christ's resurrection when the world is set aright in the end (1 Corinthians 15:20-28).

Paul's purpose in describing what happens to the dead and the living at Christ's coming is to provide counsel, reassurance, and hope rather than to predict exact future events. He is giving reasons for confident faith in Christ, even in the face of death. Paul wants the Thessalonians to know that the relationship between the believer and Christ cannot be destroyed by death. As he asserted to the Romans, nothing, not even death, can separate us from the love of God (Romans 8:38-39). "So encourage each other with these words," Paul says to the Thessalonians (1 Thessalonians 4:18).

When he writes this first letter to the Thessalonians, Paul is still working out his own understanding of death, resurrection, and the end times. His theology (understanding of God) develops throughout his life, so it is difficult to make a precise, conclusive statement about what Paul believes about the end times, particularly as he begins to understand that the end times may not arrive in his lifetime as he first thought.

What kind of hope does the church preach today? What is your hope in the Resurrection? What does the life to come look like to you? How has your theology continued to grow? Do we see ourselves as we really are in God's eyes? Think about what gives you hope in your life now and what hopes you have for life after death.

Ethical Living in the Meantime

In the final chapter of First Thessalonians, Paul continues talking about the end times (*eschaton*). He does not claim to know the time and place of the end, but calls for an ethical life in the meantime, lived faithfully and in love, in preparation for the coming of Christ. There is urgency in his message, for he too believes that Christ will return soon, when least expected, "like a thief in the night"; so believers are to remain alert. They do not want to be surprised, but rather prepared. Others who are feeling secure, and therefore not remaining alert, will be the ones who are surprised (5:1-4). Christ's coming will bless those who are watchful and ready, for they already are people of the light rather than darkness (5:4-7). Their relationship with God is already established.

In verse 8, Paul shifts to military language, calling for faith, hope, and love as armor against the unknown future, the interim until Jesus returns, fortifying Christians for the *eschaton*. God's purpose is to bring salvation, Paul says, not destruction. Then, in verse 10, Paul returns to the main point of his discussion in 4:13-18, repeating the assurance that the dead as well as the living belong to Christ.

In essence, Paul addresses the people of Thessalonica pastorally, giving them hope and providing advice about building each other up and living Christlike lives until Christ comes again to claim them. He emphasizes that living well in faith, hope, and love is the way to prepare for the coming of Christ. Paul's message provides us with a timely reminder about ethical living today as we live in the Christian way, with hope of the life to come.

Final Instructions and Blessing

The closing paragraphs of this letter include directions about respecting church leaders and being supportive of each other in the faith community, a benediction, and words of farewell.

Since at that time there were no particular offices or hierarchies in the Christian communities, leaders held the same status as everyone else. Everyone was laity. Nonetheless, leaders were needed to keep things orderly, ensure that members were cared for, and encourage and oversee the spread of the gospel. Therefore, Paul calls upon the Thessalonians to think "highly with love" of their leaders "because of their work" (5:13).

But because there was no hierarchy, Paul calls on all members to live in an orderly way and to encourage and warn everyone else as needed. At the same time, all members should live in peace with one another and care for each other.

In verse 14, Paul addresses problems causing difficulties, namely the disorderly who are excited about Christ's coming and see little need to do the work of spreading the good news, the discouraged who are worried about the status of the dead, and the weak who are making moral choices against which Paul has counseled. These difficulties may have arisen in part because of the challenges the church was facing. Skepticism about the validity of the gospel had been fueled by the death of faithful members awaiting Christ's return, because Christ was supposed to have put an end to death.

Paul calls for patience and pursuit of what is good not only for those in the community but also for those outside it (5:15). In verses 15-22, he outlines ways to encourage the growth in spirit required to meet the challenges he has discussed earlier. He calls for faith, love, and perseverance in rejoicing, praying, and giving thanks. He encourages the Thessalonians to listen with careful discernment to the Spirit-inspired interpretation of the word of God. He urges followers to pay attention to the Holy Spirit's movement and the ways Spirit-filled messages may be received.

Paul also tells his readers to hold on to what is good and avoid what is evil, which he apparently assumes they can discern for themselves, since he goes into no detail.

How do you interpret for today what it means for you to hang on to what is good and avoid what is evil? What would you consider "good" and what would you consider "evil"?

In verses 23-24, Paul adds a benediction prayer for the spirits, souls, and bodies of believers to remain blameless, holy, and therefore, sanctified for the coming of Christ. God is faithful and will answer this prayer.

Finally, Paul gives a personal word asking the church members to greet all the brothers and sisters in the church with a holy kiss. This request implies that he is addressing the whole Thessalonian church with his greeting and including them all in his prayer. He asks that the letter be read aloud, as was the custom in the churches, and that the Christians receive his blessing.

Paul spends energy and time in this letter encouraging the new church to remain steadfast and hopeful in the midst of both internal troubles and external challenges, and his message is relevant for us today. We know that Christ did not return in Paul's time and that a couple thousand years have passed. Yet, we still know that God is present with us, that Christ's teachings and saving act remains central to who we are, and that the Holy Spirit acts in us, sustaining our hope during all our days.

Live the Story

Paul's message brought hope to the persecuted church. Hope is still the good news that we Christians can bring to the world.

Name acts that you know about that bring hope to others who are hurting. Do you know of stories or movies or books that illustrate hope well? How have they affected you? How does your understanding of Christ affect your ability to hope? What sustains you?

What does the love of Christ have to do with hope? What is the power of love like? Is love necessary for hope? How do you express love and hope to others? What do you pray for when you pray for or with others, especially for those who are confused or living in despair?

What does a hope-filled life look like for you? for your family or friends? for the church? for the country? What would it take to live a hope-filled life?

What do you need to do differently now as a result of learning how Paul spoke to the Christian community about hope?

6

God's Future Speaks to Our Present

2 Thessalonians 1–3

Claim Your Story

We are in a place different from that of the early Christians. We know that Christ did not come soon after his resurrection. We know that some of the assumptions made about how God works have not played out the way that Paul thought they might. We wonder what God has in store, but do not necessarily expect that we will experience the end times in our own lifetime. We also know that God is not going to bring justice to the world the way that Paul and his followers hoped.

Our questions about faith and daily challenges are different from theirs. Because we know that Christ did not arrive with angels and fire from the clouds like the apocalyptic tradition in Paul's time indicated he would, we are left wondering how God is going to act on behalf of God's people in our own time.

Name some of the present challenges facing the earth. If the second coming of Christ occurred right now, what would happen to promote justice and peace? Would everyone be taken to Christ or would there be some left behind? Paul, in 1 Corinthians 15:21-22, says everyone will be taken to Christ; but the writer here says otherwise. Which do you believe? What do you understand about how God works in the world? What were you taught, if anything, about Christ's second coming?

But now think closer to home. Name challenges you personally face in life at the moment. It would be nice if these challenges were resolved soon, but usually you have to live with them for a time, perhaps even a long time. What do you hope God will bring to you in the future? What would seem like justice in the midst of your challenges? How can God and you work toward that justice? Does the justice include condemning someone else or someone else's actions? If so, how does that feel? If not, how might justice play out in your situation? What does peace have to do with justice?

As we enter the Bible story, think about these questions and the questions the church people in Thessalonica asked when their circumstances did not change as fast as they had hoped.

Enter the Bible Story

Introduction

Words that are particularly powerful in the letters of Paul and of his disciples include *peace, grace, hope, faith,* and *love.* We use these words often in the church, but they may mean different things to different people. For example, the writer of the second letter to the Thessalonian church uses *peace,* but it may mean "peace among you, stop bickering," or it may mean "peace of the soul." We are not sure. Likewise, speaking of God and Christ, the writer ties *grace* and *love* together (2:16). Receiving love from God is a gracious, grace-filled gift. God is not obligated to show love for us, but did so by sending Jesus to us. *Hope,* sometimes hard to feel or hang on to, comes when we learn to trust God in ways that don't make sense to our brains but we know deeply in our souls are possible and right. *Faith?* We believe in God who already believes in us.

All these words appear in Second Thessalonians, although it is not clear what specific purpose or occasion called for a second letter to the Thessalonian church. It also is not clear whether Paul wrote this second letter or if someone else did so in his name (a common practice in the ancient world). The reason for doubt is fourfold. This letter is more complex than First Thessalonians, with content and style that differ from Paul's perspective and tone in the first letter.

One discrepancy is that when the second letter discusses the end times (*eschaton*), rather than indicating that the end will come as a surprise, as Paul did in 1 Thessalonians 4–5, it urges Christians to watch for signs of its coming. The emphasis on signs comes from traditional Jewish apocalyptic thinking. In this second letter, the writer names an example of *eschatological* signs, referring specifically to a lawless ruler, likely known to the congregation, who will be punished in due course (2:3-9). The reference in verse 3 to "the rebellion" is also an example of apocalyptic thinking. It refers to forces gathering against God for a final battle before the end-time destruction. The writer indicates that this battle has not come yet, so the end is not immediate and therefore, the Thessalonians must wait patiently.

Across the Testaments

Revelation and Martyrdom

The understanding of revelation, or the unveiling of God's final acts that have already been decided, is a reversal of the present. Those who are persecuted in the present will be rewarded in the future. Those who persecute will be afflicted in the future. This attitude toward present suffering and future reward is seen in the life of martyrs, who are killed for their beliefs, but rise to glory (see Daniel 6:1-23 and also Matthew 5:10-12 for martyr theology). Often, reference to the end times (*eschaton*) uses startling imagery such as blazing fire, such as the fiery furnace in Daniel.

Another discrepancy is that the tone is different in the second letter. In the first letter, Paul consistently shows pastoral concern for the Christians in Thessalonica; in the second letter, the writing is more formal and withdrawn.

A third difficulty arises because the understanding of what happens to believers and nonbelievers after death differs in this letter from Paul's portrayal of judgment in his other letters. This letter is the only one where writing attributed to Paul speaks of God's sending nonbelievers to eternal destruction; the passage is more akin to the apocalyptic theme found in Revelation than to Paul's writings. (See Romans 14:9-12 and 2 Corinthians 5 and 10 for examples.) The statements in these letters do not indicate that those who have died after leading a life not considered faithful or righteous will be sent to eternal damnation; all Paul says is that they, along with everyone, will stand before the judgment seat. Paul's understanding of judgment differs from the writer of Second Thessalonians.

Fourth, Second Thessalonians is not authenticated as being from Paul by either a personal message or by being sent via a chosen messenger named in the letter, as Paul does in other letters. The writer attempts to appeal to handwriting (3:17) to claim authenticity, but because letters normally were dictated to scribes, the point is difficult to prove. Scholars do think that Paul adds his own hand to the end of the Colossian correspondence with a personal greeting, but he does not attempt to prove anything about authenticity, unlike here.

The conclusion? Second Thessalonians was probably written twenty-five to forty years after First Thessalonians as a way to defend Paul's stance about the second coming of Christ. The churches had been established for some time by then and Christians were struggling to understand Paul's message in terms of a Second Coming in their lifetimes. What's more, 2 Thessalonians 2:1-3 indicates that someone had spread a rumor that Paul was teaching that the day of Christ had already come, hence leading to confusion in the church.

Despite the lack of clarity about authorship, this letter is important for our study because it gives us insight into the conversations occurring about the development of Christianity in Thessalonica. Paul's followers were sent out not only to spread the good news but also to make sure that churches were remaining steadfast in times of persecution, conducting themselves in ethical ways, and answering theological questions. Letters composed by the followers of the apostles have been included in the Bible so that we understand the issues arising in the early church and see the ever-widening message of the good news. Unlike today, little distinction was made in early church times between the original writer and others writing in the writer's name. The assumption was that the message of Paul's followers was akin to what Paul taught them.

Thanksgiving and Encouragement

As in First Thessalonians, the writer begins with a greeting and thanksgiving. If we compare the two letters, we notice that the second greeting and thanksgiving is less personal. It does not discuss the relationships between Paul, his disciples, and the church. In 2 Thessalonians 1:4, the writer mentions actual persecution ("harassments and trouble"), which was more common later in the church's life than at the time Paul wrote the first letter. Persecution implies that the Christians were facing ill-treatment because of their beliefs, perhaps from government officials. The writer reassures the church that suffering makes one worthy of God's kingdom. On the other hand, those who persecute the nonbelievers will incur God's wrath at the second coming of Christ, whose arrival from heaven will include angels and blazing fire (1:7-8). Staying steadfast while being persecuted will bring reward to believers, who will come into the presence of God, while those who persecute will be separated from God (1:9-10).

The writer ends the greeting with encouragement to endure suffering with an eye toward the reward that suffering brings in the future, but he or she provides little comfort for present persecution. God, as portrayed in this letter judges nonbelievers and provides reward for the persecuted who are harassed because of their beliefs.

Second Thessalonians shows a shift occurring in how some Christians viewed God. In First Thessalonians, God is portrayed as one who comforts and cares for the Christians personally. In Second Thessalonians, the portrayal is of a God who is clear about the divide between believers and nonbelievers. It may be that this shift occurs because the letter was written later and persecution has escalated, calling for a stronger reinforcement of the teaching that God sides with believers. The shift is important to note because it shows us how the Thessalonians asked different questions as time passed, the coming of Christ was no longer expected immediately, and persecution increased. Without this letter, we would not know much about the movement of the church or its understanding of God's purpose in the world as Christianity increasingly gained a foothold as a new religion.

The Challenges of Belief

We encounter a difficult theological passage in 2:1-12. Commentators debate over meanings and interpretations, particularly over to whom the writer is referring as "lawless." The passage draws on end-time (*eschatological*) thinking in apocalyptic style. The writer is not commenting on the time and place of the *eschaton*. Instead, the writer seems to be addressing a problem in how the Thessalonians are thinking about the nature of Christian life and God's actions.

In verses 1-3, the writer states the problem that is causing a debate among those in the church. Christians are to gather prior to Christ's coming so that they can meet Christ. On one side, believers think that salvation was currently and completely available in the present because of the saving work of Jesus' resurrection already completed and the coming of the Holy Spirit already present. The other side expects that full salvation will occur when history and the cosmos come to final salvation and God's purposes are fulfilled in the *eschaton*. The first argument comes from a mix of Greek philosophy and Near Eastern mythology called Gnosticism, where Christians and others claimed a special *gnosis*, or knowledge, from Christ. The writer of the letter is trying to counter the Gnostic influence on the Thessalonian church by reinforcing that the *eschaton* is necessary for full salvation.

The writer argues against the idea of full salvation being available in the present because that would mean that Christ is not the ruler of the cosmos or history, but only of saved souls on a personal level. Further, the

About the Christian Faith

Gnosticism

Gnosis is the Greek word for "knowledge." Gnosticism was a widespread movement that had many different forms in the geographical region, but was considered a heresy stemming from Greek philosophy and Near Eastern mythology. This special knowledge, *gnosis*, from Christ claimed that baptism and Communion provided salvation for believers in the present, and there was no need for a future act by God to bring about full salvation of the world. Salvation was merely a personal concern.

writer claims that the end times are still to come, and the great rebellion against God has not occurred yet. Thus, Christians must continue to wait and be steadfast in faith. Enemies of God are already at work, but have not been allowed to do their full damage yet, because it is not time. The Thessalonians can see an example of the enemy by noting that there are those who claim their own supremacy by enthroning themselves in the Temple (verses 4-8). When it is time, the earthly agent of Satan (the lawless one) will be revealed at the same time that Christ comes. Those who have followed the deceiver will not be able to discern the truth and, therefore, will follow the false one to their own deaths (separation from God). (In the Jewish understanding of God, separation from God meant that a human being ceased to exist. Connection to God is required for existence.)

Herein lies a theological problem. The writer indicates that God sets this whole situation up. In other words, there are some people whom God predetermines will follow the lie. If God is ruler of the universe, then God is responsible for those who are deceived. Satan is allowed to work and God grants some freedom of choice, but God permits these things to occur in ways that human beings cannot understand, especially if they hold to a monotheistic notion of God (one God versus any other being equal to God, such as a Satan figure).

The church has never resolved this problem. Theology, the study of the nature of God and God's work, has a dilemma. Why would a loving God predetermine whether persons follow a lie or the truth? This question remains with us even today, usually tangled up with understandings of free will for human beings. If God gives us choices about whom and what we follow, then does God predetermine our future? The writer of this letter is clear, but we can see why questions arose in the early church about this kind of thinking, particularly among people who did not understand apocalyptic imagery and tradition.

After this heavy writing describing the *eschaton* and the nature of God (theology), the writer turns back to thanksgiving again. Believers are chosen by God and loved by God, bringing them salvation for the honor of Christ. Prayers for steadfast belief and God's encouragement of the Thessalonian Christians in their work and in their words end this section (2:13-17).

A Prayer Request and Reminders

The writer begins Chapter 3 with prayer requests including for the continued spread of the good news and the rescue from "evil people" who do not believe the good news. This reference may speak of persecution or simply of those who oppose the message. We do not know for sure. The writer does not emphasize escape from evil, but promises protection from it through Christ.

Verses 6-15 get specific about a problem in the Thessalonian church that Paul addressed in First Thessalonians. It appears that some members have persisted in idleness and undisciplined living despite Paul's earlier letter urging Christians to work hard to provide for themselves and to respect each other. The writer of Second Thessalonians is imitating Paul's concern in the first letter with one difference: this letter calls for ostracizing those who are lazy rather than admonishing them. Ostracizing them is not the same as condemning them, but it allows for dissociation from poor influences. Instead, says the writer, one is to follow Paul's example, to work for one's keep rather than expect favors. As for the loafers, they are to get to work!

Think about those who work hard at home or at church, and those who work less hard. What happens when one person becomes frustrated with another who might have a different work ethic? Does either party talk about the other outside of the home or church? Do people dissociate from each other or resent each other when this kind of conflict occurs? What kind of conversation might be helpful in these situations?

The final prayer and blessing in verses 17-18 echo First Thessalonians, with the writer again attempting to establish Pauline authenticity. Perhaps the call for peace here is especially important because of the difficulty the community is having with some of its members. The closing words invite the grace of Jesus the Christ to be with all.

Live the Story

This short letter is meant to be filled with words of encouragement for the suffering that people experience as a community of faith. In it, we find direction to look for signs of Christ's coming, when justice ultimately will prevail. The hope Christians hold is that, in God's own time, God will make right what has been corrupted by sin.

What words of encouragement based on this letter will you take away? As you think about the words that are included in greeting and farewell, namely *peace*, *grace*, *hope*, *faith*, and *love*, what do they mean to you? Give examples of how some of these words play out in your life. What about these words of encouragement or state of mind or soul lead you to make changes in your life? How might that happen? How do you expect these things to be present should there be a second coming of Christ in your lifetime?

Which of these words is most important to you personally? most important for the people you love? for the church? for the world? What would it be like to live with these words as our anchors every single day? What would happen if everyone tried to do so? How might we handle our problems if we could center in Christ's peace, grace, hope, faith, and love? Does the hope for a different kind of future, the kingdom of God on earth, help you in the present when life gets difficult?

Ultimately, the writer of Second Thessalonians assures us that God is with us in our challenges and in our journeys closer to God. That indeed is good news when life is particularly difficult! We also hear in this letter that God is aware of the faithful and the unfaithful, and a day will come when the suffering of the faithful will end. Until that time, the grace and peace of Jesus the Christ be with you now and always.

Leader Guide

People often view the Bible as a maze of obscure people, places, and events from centuries ago and struggle to relate it to their daily lives. IMMERSION invites us to experience the Bible as a record of God's loving revelation to humankind. These studies recognize our emotional, spiritual, and intellectual needs and welcome us into the Bible story and into deeper faith.

As leader of an IMMERSION group, you will help participants to encounter the Word of God and the God of the Word that will lead to new creation in Christ. You do not have to be an expert to lead; in fact, you will participate with your group in listening to and applying God's life-transforming Word to your lives. You and your group will explore the building blocks of the Christian faith through key stories, people, ideas, and teachings in every book of the Bible. You will also explore the bridges and points of connection between the Old and New Testaments.

Choosing and Using the Bible

The central goal of IMMERSION is engaging the members of your group with the Bible in a way that informs their minds, forms their hearts, and transforms the way they live out their Christian faith. Participants will need this study book and a Bible. IMMERSION is an excellent accompaniment to the Common English Bible (CEB). It shares with the CEB four common aims: clarity of language, faith in the Bible's power to transform lives, the emotional expectation that people will find the love of God, and the rational expectation that people will find the knowledge of God.

Other recommended study Bibles include *The New Interpreter's Study Bible* (NRSV), *The New Oxford Annotated Study Bible* (NRSV), *The HarperCollins Study Bible* (NRSV), the *NIV and TNIV Study Bibles*, and the *Archaeological Study Bible* (NIV). Encourage participants to use more than one translation. *The Message: The Bible in Contemporary Language* is a modern paraphrase of the Bible, based on the original languages. Eugene H. Peterson has created a masterful presentation of the Scripture text, which is best used alongside rather than in place of the CEB or another primary English translation.

One of the most reliable interpreters of the Bible's meaning is the Bible itself. Invite participants first of all to allow Scripture to have its say. Pay attention to context. Ask questions of the text. Read every passage with curiosity, always seeking to answer the basic Who? What? Where? When? and Why? questions.

Bible study groups should also have handy essential reference resources in case someone wants more information or needs clarification on specific words, terms, concepts, places, or people mentioned in the Bible. A Bible dictionary, Bible atlas, concordance, and one-volume Bible commentary together make for a good, basic reference library.

The Leader's Role

An effective leader prepares ahead. This leader guide provides easy to follow, step-by-step suggestions for leading a group. The key task of the leader is to guide discussion and activities that will engage heart and head and will invite faith development. Discussion questions are included, and you may want to add questions posed by you or your group. Here are suggestions for helping your group engage Scripture:

State questions clearly and simply.

Ask questions that move Bible truths from "outside" (dealing with concepts, ideas, or information about a passage) to "inside" (relating to the experiences, hopes, and dreams of the participants).

Work for variety in your questions, including compare and contrast, information recall, motivation, connections, speculation, and evaluation.

Avoid questions that call for yes-or-no responses or answers that are obvious.

Don't be afraid of silence during a discussion. It often yields especially thoughtful comments.

Test questions before using them by attempting to answer them yourself.

When leading a discussion, pay attention to the mood of your group by "listening" with your eyes as well as your ears.

Guidelines for the Group

IMMERSION is designed to promote full engagement with the Bible for the purpose of growing faith and building up Christian community. While much can be gained from individual reading, a group Bible study offers an ideal setting in which to achieve these aims. Encourage participants to bring their Bibles and read from Scripture during the session. Invite participants to consider the following guidelines as they participate in the group:

Respect differences of interpretation and understanding.

Support one another with Christian kindness, compassion, and courtesy.

Listen to others with the goal of understanding rather than agreeing or disagreeing.

Celebrate the opportunity to grow in faith through Bible study.

Approach the Bible as a dialogue partner, open to the possibility of being challenged or changed by God's Word.

Recognize that each person brings unique and valuable life experiences to the group and is an important part of the community.

Reflect theologically—that is, be attentive to three basic questions: What does this say about God? What does this say about me/us? What does this say about the relationship between God and me/us?

Commit to a *lived faith response* in light of insights you gain from the Bible. In other words, what changes in attitudes (how you believe) or actions (how you behave) are called for by God's Word?

Group Sessions

The group sessions, like the chapters themselves, are built around three sections: "Claim Your Story," "Enter the Bible Story," and "Live the Story." Sessions are designed to move participants from an awareness of their own life story, issues, needs, and experiences into an encounter and dialogue with the story of Scripture and to make decisions integrating their personal stories and the Bible's story.

The session plans in the following pages will provide questions and activities to help your group focus on the particular content of each chapter. In addition to questions and activities, the plans will include chapter title, Scripture, and faith focus.

Here are things to keep in mind for all the sessions:

Prepare Ahead

Study the Scripture, comparing different translations and perhaps a paraphrase.
Read the chapter, and consider what it says about your life and the Scripture.
Gather materials such as large sheets of paper or a markerboard with markers.
Prepare the learning area. Write the faith focus for all to see.

Welcome Participants

Invite participants to greet one another.
Tell them to find one or two people and talk about the faith focus.
Ask: What words stand out for you? Why?

Guide the Session

Look together at "Claim Your Story." Ask participants to give their reactions to the stories and examples given in each chapter. Use questions from the session plan to elicit comments based on personal experiences and insights.

Ask participants to open their Bibles and "Enter the Bible Story." For each portion of Scripture, use questions from the session plan to help participants gain insight into the text and relate it to issues in their own lives.

Step through the activity or questions posed in "Live the Story." Encourage participants to embrace what they have learned and to apply it in their daily lives.

Invite participants to offer their responses or insights about the boxed material in "Across the Testaments," "About the Scripture," and "About the Christian Faith."

Close the Session

Encourage participants to read the following week's Scripture and chapter before the next session.

Offer a closing prayer.

1. Jesus Christ Is the Center

Colossians 1–2

Faith Focus

Jesus Christ is the center from which our Christian life flows.

Before the Session

Read Session 1 and the first two chapters of Colossians. Gather enough hymnals for each participant to have a copy. These will be used while discussing "Hymn to Christ" below.

Claim Your Story

Invite participants to share stories about the hardest change they ever had to make and how their faith in Jesus was affected as they went through the change. Then ask participants how they define "spiritual discipline." (Be sure to explain that you mean discipline in the sense of *regimen* or *daily practice*, not in the sense of *punishment*.)

What does it mean to keep Jesus Christ in the center of your life, and why is that desirable?

How does your way of dealing with change affect your intention to stay centered on Christ?

Enter the Bible Story

Introduction and Background

Many Bible readers are surprised by and some are even troubled at suggestions that a biblical book that expressly says it is from Paul (1:1) may have been written by someone else, as the study writer indicates is possible with Colossians. Many people find it helpful to learn that in the New Testament era it was considered acceptable for coworkers of well-known teachers to write in the teacher's name, especially when the coworker intended to stay in the spirit of what the teacher taught. There may also have been times when Paul asked someone else to compose a letter in his name but gave only a broad outline of what it should include.

While we don't consider writing in someone else's name acceptable today, we do have related practices. Arthur Conan Doyle, for example, the creator of the original Sherlock Holmes books, died in 1930; but new Sherlock Holmes stories continue to be published, written by others under their own names but adhering to the spirit of the original Holmes tales.

The study writer indicates that the Colossian church members were being wooed toward a philosophy that claimed to be a purer form of Christianity than that which Paul taught. While we are less likely to encounter other philosophies in the church today, we do encounter them in our culture.

What *secular* philosophies seem appealing in our culture today? The study writer says that the topic of competing philosophies "connects for us in that the writer [of Colossians] pushes for focus on the centrality of Christ in an unfocused world that pulls people in competing directions" (page 11). How does centering on Christ help in such circumstances?

Hymn to Christ

Hand out the hymnals. Ask participants to use the hymnal index to locate a favorite hymn. Then have each person tell what *theology* (belief about God and how God works), *Christology* (belief about Christ and how Christ works), or *human faith experience* the hymn lyrics include.

Next, ask the group to turn to Colossians 1:15-20 and read together, aloud, the hymn to Christ found there. Explain that this hymn is the "heart" of the Colossian letter.

What is the *central* conviction about Jesus Christ expressed in this hymn? How might that conviction shape a Christian's life? How might it help address philosophies that go in questionable directions?

Misleading Teachings

Colossians 2:12 refers to baptism as being "buried" with Christ and then "raised" with him. In what ways does your baptism figure into your ongoing commitment to Christ? When has the fact that you are baptized caused you to make a decision or engage in an action you might not have otherwise done?

How might the fact of your baptism provide a ground from which to evaluate questionable or potentially misleading teachings?

Intention and Practice

The study writer invites us to think about how easy it is to practice religion "as a set of rules of right-living . . . without infusing our actions with a spiritual life that is sustained in Christ's love and grace" (page 16).

Where does your current practice of religion seem to be rule-driven? Does that feel as you'd like it to? What one thing could you do differently that might help you receive regular infusions of Christ's love and grace?

The notion of the "prosperity gospel" is that if we pray correctly, ask the right things of God, and live in accordance to the Scriptures, God will bless us with riches and success. In what ways is that view a distortion of faith in Christ? Why?

Is a daily devotional routine appropriate for everyone, no matter what his or her personality and appetite for change? What other ways besides a daily devotional might help people who don't respond well to routine to keep Christ in the center of their lives?

Live the Story

The various threads of this session all come together in the call to keep Christ in the center of our lives. Use the questions included in the study under the "Live the Story" section (page 17) to help participants consider once more what having Christ in the center means.

Conclude the session with prayer, asking God to help each one find the means appropriate to his or her personality to focus on Christ in the center.

2. Christ at the Center Guides Our Actions
Colossians 3–4

Faith Focus
When we are serious about living with Christ in the center, it shows in how we act.

Before the Session
In Colossians 3, the epistle writer uses a metaphor about clothing that is central to understanding the whole of Colossians. Recall that a metaphor is a comparison that is not meant literally but that helps people understand the principle or thing to which the comparison is made. The clothing metaphor is stated in 3:9-10: "Take off the old human nature with its practices and put on the new nature, which is renewed in knowledge by conforming to the image of the one who created it."

Recall, too, the limitations of metaphors. Like most teaching illustrations, this metaphor can be pushed to where it no longer supports the principle it is intended to illustrate. It's not suggesting that righteous living is something that we should put on and take off as we do our clothes. Rather, once we put on righteousness, we should continue to wear it. But the metaphor works to make the "take off" and "put on" point initially.

Claim Your Story
The last session focused on putting Christ in the center of our lives. This one takes us to the logical consequence of keeping Christ in the center: how that should manifest itself in our actions and interactions.

The study writer invites us to think about our actions especially in difficult times "even those that leave us feeling like we live in disequilibrium" (page 20). The study writer says that personal conflict is one thing that puts her in disequilibrium.

Ask the group what aspects of interactions with others they find upsetting. What kinds of interactions tend to bring forth from us unworthy or "un-Christian" responses? Does having Christ in the center make troubling interactions any easier to deal with? Does it help us respond differently from how we might otherwise?

Enter the Bible Story
Until Christ Comes
The study writer tells us that according to Pauline theology, the full Christian inheritance does not come to believers until Christ appears again and that until Christ comes, "Christians are to stay on moral ground, turn away from worldly orientation, and avoid God's

judgment by shunning wrongdoing" (page 21). This is the idea of an "interim ethic," a way of life until Christ returns.

What is the difference between a probation period and an interim ethic?

In what ways can we encourage and help one another in living that ethic?

The Clothing Metaphor

Ask participants to consider why the letter writer uses the clothing metaphor with people who have already embraced Christ. Why isn't it sufficient to simply take off the old human nature and put on a new one as a *self*-renewal project? Why must it be done as a step *after* conversion to Christ?

Remind the group of the limitations of metaphors. Holiness is not something we take on and off like clothing. But in what sense do we need to continue to improve our spiritual wardrobe?

How do we participate in the ongoing work of becoming holy? How do we set aside such things as "anger, rage, malice, slander, and obscene language" (3:8) and replace them with "compassion, kindness, humility, gentleness, and patience" (3:12)?

Does this mean we have to resist "doing what comes naturally"?

The "Clothes" of Christian Living

How does coming to church regularly and worshiping with others help with "wardrobe" adjustments?

What do you make of the study writer's statement that we are "free in Christ *not* to have to defend ourselves every time someone pushes against us" (page 24)? What about the other freedoms mentioned in the study?

Household Codes

The study writer speaks of the material in 3:18–4:1 as "household codes," that is, rules of conduct for Christians in their homes. As she indicates, the specifics of the codes don't translate directly to our culture.

How do we determine which parts of Scripture apply to us exactly as they are and which parts need to be "culturally translated"?

Ask members to read 3:18–4:1 and then summarize a single point that can be taken from those verses to be used as a directive for family life today.

Practical Advice and Greeting

The personal greetings in the letter remind us that Christianity is not a faith in isolation but a faith in community.

In what ways can the faith community be most helpful in our own ongoing work of becoming holy?

Live the Story

The study writer has provided probing questions about growing in holiness ("Live the Story," page 27). Invite group members to consider them not only in a general way, but personally. Encourage any who are willing to share their personal answers with the group to do so.

Then ask the group to stand in a circle and join hands. Pray that all who have identified needed areas of growth, whether they have shared them aloud or not, be given grace and help to progress in those areas.

3. Living God's Message
1 Thessalonians 1:1–2:16

Faith Focus

When we welcome the Holy Spirit into our lives, we embody God's message for the world.

Before the Session

Because this session is the first of three on First Thessalonians, the study writer has devoted a portion of the "Enter the Bible Story" section of this session to a general introduction of the whole book. The "Introduction and Background" section helps us understand Paul's intense concern for the Thessalonians. The "End Times" section, which is also introductory, is very helpful in understanding the mindset of the Thessalonian Christians, but has no direct bearing on the assigned passage for this session. It does apply to a topic that comes up later in the letter and will be discussed in Session 5. If your class time is short, you could omit discussion of that section, or hold it to the end, to see if time allows.

Bring a dictionary so that a volunteer can look up *embody*.

Claim Your Story

Ask for two volunteers to roleplay a short scenario where a skeptic challenges a Christian to defend the Christian faith in God in light of the corruption and tragedy in the world. The "skeptic" should play "devil's advocate" to some degree, but also be open-minded enough to give the "Christian" a fair hearing.

Afterward, ask the group how being similarly challenged about their faith would make them feel.

Next, ask if anyone present has ever felt persecuted because of Christian belief. Probably not many have, but ask participants to describe what it might be like.

What would it be like to feel called to embody God's message under such circumstances? Hand the dictionary to a volunteer and ask that person to read the definition of *embody* aloud (or have someone look it up on an iPhone or other mobile device).

What is it like to feel called to embody God's message in our circumstances, where we are seldom persecuted or challenged because of our faith?

Enter the Bible Story

Introduction and Background

Ask a volunteer to read Acts 17:1-10a to the class. Explain that this recounts the founding of the church in Thessalonica by Paul, Silas, and Timothy.

What would it feel like to help launch a church, a mission, or some other important endeavor but then be forced by circumstances to leave the work in the hands of others before it was firmly established? How would you feel about your separation from those whom the endeavor was to benefit?

End Times

Tell the group that most Christians in Paul's day (including Paul himself at the time he wrote First Thessalonians) expected the second coming of Christ to happen soon. How does our knowledge that Christ has not returned affect how we think about the end times referred to in Scripture? Do we still expect it? What do we mean by the "end times"?

Ask the group to consider the questions the study writer includes in the last paragraph of the "End Times" section of the session.

Thanksgiving and the Holy Spirit

In 1:5, Paul says that the good news (gospel) came to the Thessalonians with power, deep conviction, and the Holy Spirit. The Holy Spirit is often understood as the activity of God, the power from God that convicts, enlightens, inspires, and assures.

When have you been aware of any of those divine activities occurring in you? How does that activity of God within help you embody God's message? Can "embodying God's message" be a way of describing what it means to be "filled with the Spirit"? Why or why not?

Sources of Christianity

The study writer points out that 1:9-10 refers to two major roots of Christianity. One is monotheism, the belief in one God that Christianity carried on from the Jewish faith, the "cradle" into which Christianity was born. The other is Jesus' status as the Son of God.

Has this changed? Can Christianity be truly "Christian" without both of these?

The study writer tells us that, because the Gospels had not yet been written, Paul may have been less familiar with Jesus' work than with Jesus' status as Son of God. How does knowledge of Jesus' life and work affect how you seek to embody God's message?

God at Work in Thessalonica

Verses 2:14b-16 are "an interruption" in Paul's discussion. The study writer says that the material in those three verses may even have been a later addition, not written by Paul, and she presents evidence to support that claim. Read to the group these verses and the two paragraphs from the study guide about them (page 36).

Why can verses such as these be dangerous? How are they misused? While before his conversion Paul was himself a persecutor of Christians, would he have supported persecution of other groups after his conversion? Why or why not?

Live the Story

Ask your group to respond to the questions in the "Live the Story" section of Session 3 (page 37).

Conclude with prayer that those present might all be open to the continuing work of the Holy Spirit.

4. Travelers Who Accompany Us Enliven Our Faith
1 Thessalonians 2:17–3:13

Faith Focus
The faith of fellow travelers on the Christian journey enlivens our faith in Christ.

Before the Session
Locate a copy of the 2000 movie *Cast Away*, starring Tom Hanks. In that film, Hanks's character, Chuck Noland, becomes a solitary castaway on an island. He finds a Wilson-brand volleyball and begins speaking to it as a companion he calls "Wilson." View especially the scene where, while on a raft, Noland sees "Wilson" float away. Note how emotionally stricken Noland is. (If you have permission for a group showing, secure viewing equipment so you can play that scene for your group. Otherwise, be prepared to describe the scene to the group.)

Claim Your Story
Ask your group members if they have seen *Cast Away*. (Probably several have, as it was a popular movie.) Invite participants to describe what they remember about how the solitariness of Noland's circumstances affected him. Describe the scene when "Wilson" floated away, or play it for them.

Use the movie discussion to introduce the importance of community as described in the "Claim Your Story" section of the study. Then have your group suggest answers to the questions posed in that section.

Enter the Bible Story
Worrying About Friends
Paul was distressed because he had been forced to leave Thessalonica prematurely and especially not be on hand to help the new Christians there in their faith development.

Ask class members if any of them have ever been in a similar situation, where they had helped "birth" a new Christian but could not be available for ongoing counsel. How did that make them feel? (One example: A Christian man served at an evangelistic crusade counseling seekers who "came forward" during altar calls. The seekers came from a wide geographic area and afterward, they were referred to pastors in their own area for ongoing spiritual guidance. Still, the man was sad that he could not help guide the new converts further on the Christian journey.)

When have you wished you could be physically present with loved ones who were suffering? How did you attempt to bridge that gap?

Facing Challenges to Faith Today

The study writer speaks of Paul's concern for the suffering of the Thessalonian Christians, some of whom probably faced persecution. The study writer indicates that while few of us today ever experience persecution for our faith, we may experience skepticism from others about it or even find some people challenging our beliefs.

What effect has opposition to your faith or disinterest in your testimony had on your faith? When has a challenge to your faith caused you to think it through more clearly and learn to explain it better?

What would you say to someone who describes himself or herself as "spiritual but not religious"?

Staying Connected

Paul believes it is important to stay connected with the Thessalonian church members even though he cannot be physically present. Why?

In what ways does your church work to stay connected with members who cannot be physically present—the homebound, "snowbirds," college students, members in the armed forces, members in prison, those in mission fields? Why is it important to do so?

The Theme of Hope

In the previous section, the study writer pointed out that Paul commended the Thessalonians for their faithfulness and love (3:6), but that he said nothing about their hope. The study writer, however, said that in 3:9-13, Paul does focus on hope. Ironically, the word *hope* never appears in those verses, but the study writer is correct.

Where is hope alluded to in these verses? What does it mean to be "forward-looking" in terms of our Christian faith? Where do you find it hardest to hold on to hope? Why?

A Benediction

Verses 11-13 of Chapter 3 contain a benediction, but there is half of the letter still to go; so the placement of the benediction here seems odd.

What do you make of the study writer's suggestion that a benediction signals a transition "from one space to another"? To what "space" does the benediction in your church's worship service send you? What are the spiritual implications of that?

Invite your group to consider the questions the study writer poses in the last paragraph of the "A Benediction" section.

Live the Story

This whole session has been built on Paul's emphasis on the importance of the faith community in nurturing and enlivening the faith of each individual in the congregation. In the "Live the Story" section, the study writer has posed several questions about the faith community's role. Raise those questions with your group and allow group members to discuss them.

The goal of the lesson is *not* to give the class "something to think about" but to invite them to both rely on the strength of the faith-community and be part of that supportive community for others. So don't end with "Well, it's something to think about." End by asking class members to consider the final question in the section and then decide what specific action they are going to take as a result.

5. Life Is Hard, But Hope Is Real
1 Thessalonians 4–5

Faith Focus

Because the fullness of God's kingdom is still to come, we live with tremendous, sustaining hope.

Before the Session

Read the assigned Scripture passages and Session 5. Then go to the Internet and download the song "Life Is Hard (God Is Good)" (words and music by Pam Thum and Joel Lindsey). You should be able to find a video of it on YouTube, and the words are available on several sites. Secure a laptop on which to play the video.

Claim Your Story

Begin your session by playing the video of "Life Is Hard (God Is Good)." Then ask members to tell in what ways the words of the song describe life as they know it.

After that discussion, ask participants to consider the questions in the "Claim Your Story" section of the study.

Then read to them the final paragraph of the "Claim Your Story" section.

Enter the Bible Story
Living a Holy Life

The study writer reminds us that at the time Paul penned his letter to the Thessalonians, the Gospels had not yet been written, meaning that "Paul had little of Jesus' teaching tradition from which to draw" (page 50). Ask your group to tell how much they would understand about Jesus' message and work if the Gospels did not exist.

What Paul did have, however, was his personal conversion experience, in which he heard Jesus in a vision, and the testimony and personal accounts from the apostles and others who had been with Jesus in the days of his human life.

In what ways has your personal experience of Christ helped you decide what is right and what is wrong in daily living?

In what ways have fellow worshipers assisted you in ethical living?

The study writer also tells us that Paul was concerned about the reputation of the church "in a world that thinks it suspect in the first place" (page 52). Where in our society today is the church thought to be "suspect"?

Ask class members to read the last two paragraphs in the "Living a Holy Life" section and to respond to the questions there.

Death and Resurrection

The Thessalonian Christians were concerned about what would be the fate of the faithful who had already died before Christ returned. Do the concerns of the Thessalonian Christians connect with your group members? Encourage your group to discuss what comes to mind when they hear the term *Second Coming.* Do you still expect an actual Second Coming with the kinds of happenings Paul described in 1 Thessalonians 4:16-17?

The study writer points out that Paul was still working out his understanding of all of this and that his conclusions underwent revisions as time passed.

In what ways are hope and the coming of God's kingdom connected?

Ethical Living in the Meantime

While Paul wrote to the Thessalonians about the end times, which he still expected to occur in the near future, he also called on them to live ethically in the meantime. They were to live prepared, so that no matter when Christ returned, they would be ready and have nothing about which to be ashamed.

Given that our whole lives to this date have been in that "meantime," how do Paul's instructions apply to us? In what ways does "living in the meantime" affect hope? affect faith? affect our willingness to engage in good works? Why?

Final Instructions and Blessing

Ask a volunteer to read 5:15-22. Then invite the group to discuss how those verses apply to the Christian life in our age.

Paul found it necessary to address problems within the church caused by the disorderly, the discouraged, and those making poor moral choices (5:14). In what ways does your church try to help people overcome those issues today?

What helps you avoid evil?

What helps you "hang on to what is good"?

Live the Story

Paul's letter to the Thessalonians brought hope to Christians in hard times. Hope is still a crucial element today.

Ask class members to consider the questions the study writer included in the "Live the Story" section.

Then ask participants to look at the title of "Life Is Hard (God Is Good)." Why do you think the songwriters included both phrases in the title? What does the message "Life Is Hard" lack? What's missing when we proclaim only that "God Is Good"? How does the combination of the two phrases describe hope?

Conclude with prayer for all those in your congregation who are experiencing difficult times.

6. God's Future Speaks to Our Present
2 Thessalonians 1–3

Faith Focus

We are better able to deal with our present difficulties and problems when we consider them in the light of God's future.

Before the Session

The circumstances and concerns of those in Thessalonica who received the letter we call Second Thessalonians were quite different from our circumstances and concerns. Yet because we Christians consider all Scripture profitable not only for study but also for hearing God's message for us, it's important that we listen for the larger themes in Second Thessalonians.

So, as you read Second Thessalonians in preparation for teaching, look for the broader concerns behind the immediate issues of the Thessalonians. (Some of those concerns are summed up in the Faith Focus statement above.)

Arrange for a whiteboard or newsprint and markers to use in the "Introduction" portion of the "Enter the Bible Story" section.

Claim Your Story

Begin by telling your group that the circumstances and concerns of the Thessalonians at the time of the second letter to that church are quite different from our own. By way of introduction, you might mention the following:

- The Thessalonians were being persecuted; we are not.
- They were rethinking their faith in light of the realization that Christ wasn't returning as quickly as they had expected; we haven't had those "any day now" expectations to start with.
- They were dealing with "undisciplined" members; we tend to leave undisciplined members to work out their own way forward.
- They expected negative circumstances to resolve quickly because of Christ's return; we tend to think in terms of dealing with some negative issues over the "long-haul" of life.

Next, ask class members to consider the questions the study writer has posed in the "Claim Your Story" section.

Enter the Bible Story

Introduction

The study writer says that Second Thessalonians uses the words *peace, grace, hope, faith,* and *love* but that it is not always clear how they are meant to be applied in the Thessalonian church. List these five words on a whiteboard or on newsprint, and ask participants to supply definitions of how they would expect those words to be used in the church. Then ask them to indicate how they seemed to be used in the following contexts in Second Thessalonians:

- peace — 1:2; 3:16
- grace — 1:2; 2:16; 3:18
- hope — 2:16
- faith (faithfulness) — 1:3; 1:4; 1:11; 3:2
- love — 1:3; 2:10; 2:16; 3:5

The introductory section devotes several paragraphs to the matter of who wrote Second Thessalonians, explaining that the letter may have been the work of a disciple of Paul's, writing in the apostle's name. (This was an accepted practice in the first century.)

Since the early church considered the letter Scripture, does it matter who actually penned it? Is the designation as "Scripture" sufficient for us to take the words seriously?

Read to the group the last paragraph in the "Introduction" section.

Thanksgiving and Encouragement

The study writer indicates that Second Thessalonians shows a shift occurring in how some Christians viewed God (shifting from how First Thessalonians portrays their view). Ask a volunteer to read aloud the final paragraph in the "Thanksgiving and Encouragement" section. Then ask class members to consider whether maturing faith naturally sees God in new ways. What circumstances cause us to develop inadequate views of God? What circumstances cause us to broaden our views of God? How does the Bible help in that process?

The Challenges of Belief

The study writer rightly tells us that 2:1-12 is a difficult passage theologically, and she goes on to explain the difficulty in terms of the timing of *full* salvation—as a gift already given when one accepts Christ versus a gift that only occurs at the end times (the *eschaton*). This is a debate that today's church seldom addresses, for the understanding of full salvation being granted at the time one accepts Christ is now a commonly accepted doctrine. But the airing of the debate in Thessalonica is useful as a model of how the early church sorted through its beliefs and arrived at common understandings.

How does the promise of God's future, regardless of the details about it, help us with present difficulties and problems?

This section also mentions other theological issues, at least one of which is still not fully resolved. What does it mean to hold a faith where not every question is answered? To what degree is your personal experience of faith always a "work in progress"?

A Prayer Request and Reminders

Second Thessalonians 3:6-15 offers advice for dealing with undisciplined members. Read those verses aloud and discuss how the principles behind them should be applied to our life as members together today. When have *you* been among the "undisciplined"?

Live the Story

Invite participants to respond to the questions included in the "Live the Story" section of the study.

The final sentence of the study is a benediction. Ask members what it means to them when a leader or member uses a benediction to bless them.

Conclude the session with the benediction in that final sentence.